The National Poetry Series

The National Poetry Series was established in 1978 to publish five collections of poetry annually through five participating publishers. The manuscripts are selected by five poets of national reputation. Publication is funded by James A. Michener, Edward J. Piszek, The Ford Foundation, The Witter Bynner Foundation, and the five publishers—Doubleday, E. P. Dutton, Harper & Row, Random House, and Holt, Rinehart & Winston.

The National Poetry Series—1980

Sterling A. Brown, COLLECTED POEMS (Selected by Michael S. Harper)
Joseph Langland, ANY BODY'S SONG (Selected by Ann Stanford)
Ronald Perry, DENIZENS (Selected by Donald Justice)
Wendy Salinger, FOLLY RIVER (Selected by Donald Hall)
Roberta Spear, SILKS (Selected by Philip Levine)

Books by Sterling A. Brown

Poetry
SOUTHERN ROAD

THE LAST RIDE OF WILD BILL

Criticism
OUTLINE FOR THE STUDY OF
THE POETRY OF AMERICAN NEGROES

THE NEGRO IN AMERICAN FICTION

NEGRO POETRY AND DRAMA

Other
THE NEGRO IN WASHINGTON (EDITOR)

THE NEGRO IN VIRGINIA (EDITOR)

THE NEGRO CARAVAN (EDITOR)

The Collected Poems of Sterling A. Brown

selected by Michael S. Harper

HARPER COLOPHON BOOKS

HARPER & ROW, PUBLISHERS

NEW YORK, CAMBRIDGE, PHILADELPHIA, SAN FRANCISCO

LONDON, MEXICO CITY, SAO PAULO, SYDNEY

Grateful acknowledgment is made for permission to reprint:

"All Are Gay" from *American Stuff*. Copyright 1937 by The Guild's Committee for Federal
  Writers' Publications. Reprinted by permission of Viking Penguin, Inc.
"An Old Woman Remembers" originally appeared in *Freedomways*.
"Bitter Fruit of the Tree" originally appeared in *The Nation*.
"Glory, Glory" originally appeared in *Esquire*.
"Master and Man" originally appeared in *The New Republic*.
"Transfer" and "Southern Cop" originally appeared in *Partisan Review*.
"The Young Ones" originally appeared in *Poetry*.

Southern Road by Sterling Brown. Copyright 1932 by Harcourt, Brace & Co. Copyright renewed
1960 by Sterling Brown.

"An Annotated Bibliography of The Works of Sterling Brown" by permission of Robert G.
O'Meally.

A hardcover edition of this book is published by Harper & Row, Publishers, Inc.

First HARPER COLOPHON edition published 1983.

Library of Congress Cataloging in Publication Data

Brown, Sterling Allen, 1901–
     The collected poems of Sterling A. Brown.

     (Harper colophon books ; CN/1016)
     Bibliography: p.
     I. Harper, Michael S.   II. Title.
PS3503.R833A17   1983   811'.52   82-48230
ISBN 0-06-091016-X (pbk.)

83 84 85 86 10 9 8 7 6 5 4 3 2 1

To Rose Anne, as ever

Contents

Part Three: TIN ROOF BLUES

Part Four: VESTIGES

THE LAST RIDE OF WILD BILL

NO HIDING PLACE

Preface

The publication of Sterling Brown's *Collected Poems* is an historical event, and it is also a personal triumph, another instance of Brown's "jumping the gap of the generations," for his poems have always been very demanding on the senses, *and* on the intellect; though he has never been a poet of fashion, this collection secures his rightful place at the center of American letters. His career embodies literary and critical values, scholarship, and political astuteness; many of his poems embody the tension between the private and public visions of a people's aspirations, disappointments, triumphs, and a durability summed up in the title of Brown's rejected second book of poems, *No Hiding Place:*

> Went down to the rocks to hide my face,
> The rocks cried out no hiding place.

The practical lessons of poetic composition are widely displayed in this volume, and though the content is moving, often focusing on characters locked in mortal struggle of life and limb in the name of those heroic values, dignity and equality and great sacrifice, Brown's *consciousness* and *conscientiousness* of craft and technique are experimental, innovative, and deepened in a wide body of formal undertakings in the nature and balance of the artistic act. His poems are *made,* born of vision and revision, as a sculptor chisels, and Brown does, or a painter paints; biography is not poetry, but poetry demands a life fully lived—the poem is the performance. Sterling Brown's sense of design, of composition as a rigorous discipline, instructs and informs and extends a continuous consciousness of history and literary form. His own heroic ideal—*been down so long that down don't worry me*—is an abiding commitment to the word made flesh. His poetry teaches in the sense that it illustrates a clarity and precision of form as the skeletal structure of the expressive designs of language, and that language has a purity of diction because the poet's selectivity is the voice of authority—he controls the atmosphere, cadence, and pace of utterance, activating the landscape and voicings of the poem, while disarming his reader, his hearer. Brown's poems are deceptively literate; they move as images created and controlled as activation, as an agency of contact; in this sense he is a great poet of community. Brown's world is grounded in his perceptual faith in the long haul, and in the spirit which needs no hiding. In the words of his mythical hero, John Henry:

John Henry said to his captain,
        "A man ain't nothin' but a man,
But before I'll let dat steam drill beat me down,
        I'll die wid my hammer in my hand,
                Die wid my hammer in my hand."

Sterling Brown is a trustee of consciousness, and a national treasure; he will die with *that* hammer in his hand. His poems now belong to us all.

MICHAEL S. HARPER

Brown University
October 1979

SOUTHERN ROAD

Introduction

Unlike the others, the poet had not introduced himself. He had simply said, "Ma Rainey," and continued in a way that indicated an unusual affinity between author and poem, between voice and word. It seemed the most natural and impressive delivery I had ever heard:

> I talked to a fellow, an' the fellow say,
> "She jes' catch hold of us, some kindaway.
> She sang Backwater Blues one day . . .
>
> "An' den de folks, dey natchally bowed dey heads an' cried,
> Bowed dey heavy heads, shet dey moufs up tight an' cried,
> An Ma lef' de stage, an' followed some de folks outside."

And then those lines which say so much, which enable one to *feel* so much, about the great Blues singer and her followers:

> Dere wasn't much more de fellow say:
> She jes' gits hold of us dataway.

It was a weekend in the summer of '62 at a resort near Detroit, just on the other side of the Canadian border. We were listening to a recording being amplified throughout the grounds of poets reading their works. Just standing at that early hour on a Sunday morning would have been, under most circumstances, an achievement, but this time I was startled upright and determined to get to the record player to discover whose voice it was. The voice belonged to Sterling A. Brown. I wondered then and later how a Williams College Phi Beta Kappa, a Harvard man, a college professor, and eminent writer could have a voice with so much of earth and sky and sunlight and dark clouds about it; a voice unafraid, an instrument Blues-tinged.[1]

With W. E. B. Du Bois in Ghana, Brown was even then the Dean of American Negro scholars, a man noted especially for his brilliant defenses of Negro character in literature. But for decades he had operated almost exclusively on the Howard campus, and there was some reason to wonder whether the Negro literati at Howard and at other centers of learning had much conception of why he was important, apart from the fact that he was known to be a man of learning with a rather inexplicable interest in Blues, Jazz, and Negro Spirituals. Even then—especially then, for it was at the height of the Civil Rights Movement—one sensed in Sterling Brown's voice a connecting timbre, a feel for reciprocity between past and present.

If listened to, if called upon, some of us thought he could speak to the spiritual state of his people. But civil rights leaders were not overly interested in matters of culture or heritage.[2] And members of the black bourgeoisie were scarcely in the mood to seek counsel from poets, especially from one who might speak of slavery and provide a glimpse of a future which, even in freedom, would not be easy. Besides, the sixties seemed to belong to younger, "angrier" writers.

Later in 1962 Sterling Brown lectured on folklore for Chicago's Amistad Society and made a big impression on hundreds of people on the South Side. After his lecture before a small group, he read poems until daybreak —from a sheaf of yellowed pages, some of them tattered at the edges— poems never before anthologized, poems not found in *Southern Road*—and they did not appear to be the least dated.

After his lecture and poetry reading (his first in Chicago), Brown returned several times—"my best audiences are in Chicago," he has said. Each time, whatever the age group or racial composition of the audience, his reading was singularly successful, which buoyed his spirits, for he had in fact wondered perhaps more than he ever let us know how the younger generation would relate to his poetry.[3] It was evident that despite his great gifts as a poet, he was troubled by a not inconsiderable lack of recognition. Those who knew and respected him assumed that he had fallen silent, had stopped writing poetry, shortly after the appearance of *Southern Road*. That assumption, together with sadly deficient criticism from some quarters, helped to fix his place in time—as a not very important poet of the past.[4]

A man who has gone his own way most of his life, Brown has not been noted for asking favors, for seeking the easy way out by playing games with critics or with other people of influence. Among his favorite lines are these from Robert Frost's "In Dives' Dive":

> It is late at night and still I am losing,
> But still I am steady and unaccusing.

However, Sterling Brown was once taken far more seriously than he is today—and by critics who had done their homework. That was roughly forty years ago, and those critics had offered high praise.

I

Alain Locke, perhaps the chief aesthetician of the New Negro Movement and clearly its most effective defender, acknowledged that numerous critics, on the appearance of *Southern Road*, had hailed Brown "as a significant new Negro poet." For Locke, that was not sufficient: "The discriminating few go further; they hail a new era in Negro poetry, for such is the deeper significance of this volume." Locke identified the principal objective of Negro poetry "as the poetic portrayal of Negro folk-life," suggested that such portraits should be "true in both letter and spirit to the idiom of the folk's own way of feeling and thinking," and declared that with the publication of *Southern Road* it could be said "that here for the first time is that much-desired and long-awaited acme attained or brought within actual reach."[5] As the folk-poet of the new Negro, Brown was for Locke the most important of Negro poets. This folk-poet appellation was an appropriate one, for Brown had recognized and begun to mine the rich veins of Negro folklore and found there almost boundless artistic possibilities for exploring the human condition.

Not meaning to ascribe perfection and complete maturity to Brown's art, Locke described him as "a Negro poet with almost complete detachment, yet with a tone of persuasive sincerity, whose muse neither clowns nor shouts. . . ." In Locke's view Brown had been able to create with the naturalness and freshness integral to folk balladry, and he called attention to "Maumee Ruth," "Sam Smiley," "Dark of the Moon," "Johnny Thomas," "Slim Greer," and "Memphis Blues" as convincing proof that a Negro poet could "achieve an authentic folk-touch."[6]

Locke was fond of "Maumee Ruth," a poem in which Brown, as he did on a number of occasions, linked North and South, countryside and city; a poem which Locke considered as uniquely racial as "Southern Road," the title poem with work-song rhythms:

> White man tells me—hunh—
> Damn yo' soul;
> White man tells me—hunh—
> Damn yo' soul;
> Got no need, bebby,
> To be tole.

In Locke's opinion a number of Negro poets had been too reluctant to show their own people in a truer light, though they had become increasingly bold and now were no longer "too gingerly and conciliatory to and about the white man. The Negro muse weaned itself of that in McKay, Fenton Johnson, Toomer, Countée Cullen and Langston Hughes. But in Sterling Brown it has learned to laugh at itself and to chide itself. . . ."[7] Locke considered Brown a finer student of folk-life, more thoughtful, more detached, more daring than the others. Here was a poet who had gone further still and had explored, "with deeply penetrating genius," fundamental and abiding qualities of Negro feeling and thought, establishing "a sort of common denominator between the old and the new Negro."[8]

Louis Untermeyer, in a review of *Southern Road,* warned against ranking other poets of the New Negro Movement with Brown. But for those who "insist that such strains have been played before by the darker-minded of Brown's race, I would reply that Brown achieves a detachment which Claude McKay, for all his ardor, or Countée Cullen, for all his fluency, never achieves."[9] Untermeyer, in his appreciation of Brown's detachment, pointed to one of Brown's characteristics which should be pondered by many of the new black poets. Brown's mastery of a first principle of his craft: the poet should not shout or scream but, through singular command of language, perspective, mood, and event, win his way toward triggering a desire to shout *in the reader.* Brown's detachment, according to Untermeyer, allows him "to expostulate without ranting, or even raising his voice. . . ." "Only the most purblind—or prejudiced—will refuse to admit," thought Untermeyer, the strength and power of *Southern Road.*[10]

While he found "Odyssey of Big Boy" and "Frankie and Johnny" not to his liking, Untermeyer considered *Southern Road* as a whole "not only suffused with the extreme color, the deep suffering and high laughter of workers in cabins and cottonfields, of gangs and gutters, but it vibrates with a less obvious glow—the glow which, however variously it may be defined, is immediately perceived and ultimately recognized as poetry."[11] "Brown," Untermeyer concluded, "has expressed sources and depths which a pioneer like Dunbar might have felt but could never voice. . . . Thus 'Southern Road' reveals old material and a new utterance. Another light has emerged from the dark, unexhausted mine."[12]

The reviewer for *The New Republic* praised Brown for genuine originality in handling folk materials, noted the absence of pretension in his work, and hailed his "forthright use of realistic Negro material" as a characteristic worthy of emulation by those following him.[13] The reviewer for *The Nation* shrewdly realized that Brown's poems on the folk Negro experience were not conventional dialect renderings of that reality but were written in the natural, vigorous speech of the contemporary Negro. *The Nation* critic had put his finger on an aspect of Brown's poetry that has been misunderstood by a number of critics.[14]

That Brown's treatment of the folk Negro was destitute of maudlin sentimentality and outlandish humor, hallmarks of most traditional dialect poetry, was altogether clear to William Rose Benét. Commenting on *Southern Road* in the *Saturday Review of Literature,* Benét also called the reader's attention to Brown's qualities as a narrative poet: "The fact that Brown is so good a narrative poet has inclined me toward him," he wrote. Benét found a command of real pathos and grimness in Brown's treatment of "Sam Smiley," the buckdancer and veteran of foreign wars who, on returning home, put to use, without, color discrimination, his martial skills; Sam Smiley, who in the end:

Buckdanced on the midnight air.

Brown's ability to "strike out original simile," as in "Tornado Blues" (from "New St. Louis Blues"):

Black wind come a-speedin' down de river from de Kansas plains,
Black wind come a-speedin' down de river from de Kansas plains,
Black wind come a-roarin' like a flock of giant aeroplanes—

impressed the reviewer. Benét also considered "peerless" some of the verses in the three "Slim Greer" poems, a series in which he thought humorous Negro fables were related with "inimitable unction."[15]

In several Slim Greer stanzas, Brown shows the reader how the suggestive powers of language can call reality into play with uncommon force, revealing terrible potential for turbulence beneath mirth that is in the final analysis no more than surface deep. Slim Greer seeking to pass for white romancing the Southern white woman was faced with an especially deadly moment of racial truth when his love

Crept into the parlor
Soft as you please
Where Slim was agitatin'
The ivories.

Heard Slim's music—
An' then, hot damn!
Shouted sharp—"Nigger!"
An' Slim said, "Ma'am?"

And the reviewer found, in the last section of *Southern Road,* "Thoughts of Death," "Against That Day," and the sonnet "Rain" to be "entirely uncolloquial . . . unusually well-fashioned." The overall estimate was glowing: Brown's work had "distinctly more originality and power than that of Countée Cullen, and more range than that of Langston Hughes." Of the younger Negro poets, he closed, "I consider Sterling A. Brown to be the most versatile and the least derivative."[16]

The *New York Times* printed a lengthy review of *Southern Road* which also drew attention to the E. Simms Campbell illustrations. The reviewer found race on every page, "but it is 'race' neither arrogant nor servile. There is pathos, infinite pathos; but everywhere there is dignity that respects itself." The reviewer, unafraid of Negro bitterness, called the reader's attention to "Maumee Ruth," finding in it sentiments that have been expressed "from the earliest poetry of the Hebrews down to the present day." He also trenchantly observed that the gayety found in *Southern Road* is "on the whole gayety restrained."[17] One must differ with the assertion that race

7

is on every page, but that objection is little more than quibbling since race is indeed prominent in *Southern Road*. The *New York Times* review could scarcely have offered a finer tribute, one worth quoting in full: "*Southern Road* is a book the importance of which is considerable. It not only indicates how far the Negro artist has progressed . . . but it proves that the Negro artist is abundantly capable of making an original and genuine contribution to American literature . . . there is everywhere art, such a firm touch of artistry as is only seldom found among poets of whatever descent."[18]

That James Weldon Johnson introduced *Southern Road* when it first appeared in 1932 suggests something of the powerful effect which Sterling Brown's poetry had upon him. Perhaps by then Johnson had realized that, while his earlier strictures about dialect poetry had been correct enough when applied to the verse of others, they were simply not applicable to the poetry of Sterling Brown. Citing Brown's use of ballads and folk epics, he suggests that when the raw material upon which the poet works is radically different from the excessive geniality and optimism, the sentimentality and artificiality found in poetry based on the minstrel tradition, one is on the threshold of a breakthrough in poetic experimentation and achievement. Brown, Johnson tells us, mastered the spirit of his materials to the point of absorption and, "adopting as his medium the common, racy, living speech of the Negro in certain phases of *real* life," re-expressed that spirit with artistry and greater power.

If my reading of Johnson is correct, then his statement that "Mr. Brown's work is not only fine, it is also unique" is all the more comprehensible. Unique as well, Johnson correctly notes, are many of Sterling Brown's poems, which "admit of no classification or brand, as, for example, the gorgeous 'Sporting Beasley.'" In that poem, the "Slim Greer" cycle, and in others, Johnson added, "[Brown] gives free play to a delicious ironical humor that is genuinely Negro." Johnson ventured to classify "Sporting Beasley," calling it "Sterling-Brownian." He concluded his remarks with the observation that while there are "excellent poems written in literary English and form" in *Southern Road* "it is in his poems whose sources are the folk life that [Brown] makes, beyond question, a distinctive contribution to American poetry."

And so it was a remarkable achievement for a young poet: not one of the major reviewers hailed Brown as a poet of promise, as a talented young man awaiting creative maturity; on the contrary, he was regarded as a poet of uncommon sophistication, of demonstrated brilliance whose work had placed him in the front rank of working poets here and elsewhere. And the critics had been correct in noting that the maturity of Sterling Brown's poetic vision, the success with which he focused and ranged it over the varied terrain of Southern Negro experience, venturing now and again into higher latitudes such as Chicago, was not a result of unpracticed, intuitive genius. To be sure, most of Brown's years before the completion of his manuscript were helpful in preparing him for *Southern Road*.

II

In ways both subtle and obvious Sterling Nelson Brown, distinguished minister and father of the poet, influenced his son's attitude toward life and literature. Born a slave in eastern Tennessee, the elder Brown, unlike many of similar origin, was not ashamed of his slave heritage, nor was he ashamed of rural Negro descendants of slaves. The sense of continuity with the past and the considerable attention devoted to the folk Negro in Brown's poetry probably owe as much to his having been the son of such a father as they do to the valuable experiences which the young poet had in the South following his graduation from Williams College and Harvard University.[19]

Fortunately Sterling A. Brown, exposed to the critical realist approach to literature of George Dutton of Williams and the realism that characterized some of the best of American poetry of the twenties, especially the work of Edwin Arlington Robinson, Robert Frost, and Carl Sandburg, was all the more prepared to take an uncondescending, that is to say genuinely respectful, attitude toward the folk whom he encountered in the South. And there he discovered a wealth of folk material waiting to be fashioned into art, and a number of quite ordinary people who, thanks to his artistry, would teach us unusual things about life. Brown realized the need to explore the life of the Southern Negro below the surface in order to reveal unseen aspects of his being, his strength and fortitude, his healing humor, and his way of confronting tragedy. As a young man he began meeting and talking to a variety of people, some of whom, such as Big Boy Davis, a traveling guitar player after whom the character in "Southern Road," the title poem, is modeled, would win permanent places in our literature. The fact that Brown, with his sharp eye, fine ear, and excellent mind, spent so many of his early years in the South helps us understand the sensibility behind a volume which reads like the work of a gifted poet who has lived a lifetime.

Just as Brown's creation of folk characters presents individualized portraits revelatory of interior lives, his uses of the great body of Negro music, of the Spirituals, Blues, Jazz, and Work Songs, extend rather than reflect meanings. Sadly enough, there is reason to believe that many students of Negro literature, as I have implied, are unfamiliar with most of the poems in *Southern Road*. Numerous major poems have never been anthologized; and some, such as "Cabaret," have only recently been brought to our attention by critics.[20] Yet a specialist on the "Harlem Renaissance," of which Brown was not a part, *places him in that movement* with a number of references, including one to "Memphis Blues," while omitting mention of "Cabaret," perhaps the single most important New Negro Movement poem dealing with the exploitation of Negro performing artists, especially members of orchestras and chorus lines, during the twenties and since.[21]

Though "Cabaret" is by no means the only significant Brown poem that numerous scholars don't seem to know exists, it deserves attention because of its brilliant multi-level interplay between appearance and reality: between life as Negroes live it and life as projected onto them by white audiences. "Cabaret" stands as a starkly eloquent emblem of the frustrations, cleverly masked, of Negro entertainers before the bizarre expectations of white patrons of black arts of the twenties. The inexorably grim logic of the poem unfolds to the accompaniment of Negro music in a Chicago Black and Tan club in 1927. The poet employs symbolically the Blues, Jazz, the corruptions of Tin Pan Alley, the perversions of genuine Negro music, the dirty misuse of Negro chorus girls and musicians—all set against the rural tragedy of a desperate people in the terrible flood of 1927.

Though I had the rare pleasure of hearing Brown recite the following lyrical, gut-bucket stanzas—recite them magnificently—to my knowledge "Kentucky Blues" has never been anthologized:

> I'm Kentucky born,
> Kentucky bred,
> Gonna brag about Kentucky
> Till I'm dead.
>
> . . .
>
> Ain't got no woman,
> Nor no Man O' War,
> But dis nigger git
> What he's hankering for—
>
> De red licker's good,
> An' it ain't too high,
> Gonna brag about Kentucky
> Till I die. . . .

The narrator of "Kentucky Blues" would be completely at home in "Memphis Blues," whose last grim stanza closes with a brilliantly conceived reference to another art form, not unknown for qualities of stoicism, to the mood of the poem:

> Memphis go
> By Flood or Flame;
> Nigger don't worry
> All de same—

> Memphis go
> Memphis come back,
> Ain' no skin
> Off de nigger's back.
> All dese cities
> Ashes, rust. . . .
> De win' sing sperrichals
> Through deir dus'

As a student of the relationship between past and present, of the effects of time and circumstance upon human beings, Sterling Brown has demonstrated, as well as any artist known to this writer, how music and myth function in the lives of ordinary people. In but a portion of a single stanza from "Ma Rainey," perhaps *the* Blues poem, Brown manages to capture in a few lean lines the essence of the Blues singer as repository, as explicator of the values of her people, as Priestess.

> O Ma Rainey,
> Sing yo' song;
> Now you's back
> Whah you belong,
> Git way inside us,
> Keep us strong. . . .

And in "Strange Legacies," we encounter perhaps the greatest of all Negro folk heroes:

> Brother,
> When, beneath the burning sun
> The sweat poured down and the breath came thick,
> And the loaded hammer swung like a ton
> And the heart grew sick;
> You had what we need now, John Henry.
> Help us get it.
>
> *So if we go down*
> *Have to go down*
> *We go like you, brother,*
> *'Nachal' men. . . .*

But in "Children's Children" the poet turns to discontinuities, to a poignant breakdown in racial memory:

> When they hear
> These songs, born of the travail of their sires,

> Diamonds of song, deep buried beneath the weight
> Of dark and heavy years;
> They laugh.
>   . . .
> They have forgotten, they have never known,
> Long days beneath the torrid Dixie sun
>   . . .
> With these songs, sole comfort.

As remarkable as many of the poems in this volume are, they can, like arresting but isolated portions of a vast canvas, be done full justice only when seen within the framework of the overall artistic conception. This is so because Sterling Brown, despite the impressive range of characterization and technique revealed in this volume, builds from a unified, integrated conception of reality. The happy effect of such architecture is that individual poems, however much they dazzle when read apart from others, gain new and deeper meaning, and a new resonance, when the entire volume is read.

Given the experiences of his people in America, it is especially worth noting that Brown has been able to take attributes that appear greatly susceptible to stereotypical treatment—cheating, flight, laughing, dancing, singing—and, never losing control of them, in fact utilizing them repeatedly, to establish the irreducible dignity of a people. So powerful is his vision of their humanity, so persuasive his powers of poetic transmutation, that his utilization of the most distinctly Negroid accents serves to enlarge, rather than diminish, that humanity. In a word, Brown makes no concessions to white prejudice or to Negro pretense.

If Sterling Brown speaks of tragedy, he also holds out the ultimate hope of triumph, the possibility of which, paradoxically, is heightened, not lessened, by the tough-minded quality of his way of reckoning events and determining what is important in life. His disclosures of largely unappreciated qualities, though they range over myriad concerns, are on balance values, sacred and secular, hidden in the hearts of a people. "Strong Men" gives us a better sense of what the long haul has meant, of how a people has not merely survived but projected its sense of what is meaningful, than any other poem in Afro-American literature. The vision which informs this poem is essentially the same which courses through a volume offering no easy optimism and no quick victories but all the determination in the world. And so there is a promise of eventual relief. The poet's vision is, in the end, tragic—triumphant.

In spite of all, whatever his setbacks, whatever his triumphs, Sterling Brown has maintained through it all possession of his soul and kept the faith with his fellows, living and dead. He is an artist in the truest sense:

the complete man, he has attempted to master the art of living. One is reminded, when thinking of him, of Lionel Trilling's reference to certain "men who live their visions . . . who *are* what they write."[22]

As Sterling Brown reveals the world of *Southern Road,* he leads us ultimately, through the Negro, to a conception of the nature of man. There is a noticeable absence of the questionable poetic ideal of being "difficult," which too frequently has come to mean, in our time, impenetrability. Yet Brown's genius is such that as he sculpts simple, plain speech into poetry, as he unveils the value ensemble of a people, the reader will discover, almost in a flash, that he has entered a world as wondrously complex as life itself.

STERLING STUCKEY

Evanston, Illinois
April 1974

NOTES

1. Sterling A. Brown was born in Washington, D.C., in 1901. He has taught at Virginia Seminary, at Lincoln University (Missouri), at Fisk, and, since 1929, at Howard University. From 1936 to 1939 he was Editor of Negro Affairs for the Federal Writers' Project. He was also a staff member of the Carnegie-Myrdal Study of the Negro. He has, in addition to having authored scores of scholarly articles, published *The Negro in American Fiction* (1938), *Negro Poetry and Drama* (1938), and, with Ulysses Lee and Arthur P. Davis, edited the noted anthology *The Negro Caravan* (1941). A collection of Brown's essays, *A Different Drummer,* is being readied for publication by Howard University Press.

2. A number of leading figures in SNCC were interested in cultural questions. Mike Thelwell, Charlie Cobb, Stokely Carmichael, Bill Mahoney, and Courtland Cox—all students of Brown at Howard—possessed more than a little knowledge of the folk heritage of Afro-America, which was not altogether unrelated to that consciousness within SNCC which led to the call for black power.

3. Actually, few people relate to younger people as well as Sterling Brown, who somehow, despite his age, does not seem "old." Hoyt Fuller, editor of *Black World,* has captured a number of Brown's qualities: "Settle him down, loosen his tie, provide him with some congenial and intelligent company, and turn him on. The stories flow. Out of his fascinating past, a life filled with both raw and genteel adventures in that mad, rich, vibrant world on the mellow sidelines of America, he serves up a living history of the past forty years. . . . Who are the others who can sit among a roomful of men and women young enough to be their children and meld in spirit and mood with no hint of pomp and no suggestion of paternalism? . . . His books are where the minds are which have been touched by his vivid stories,

13

his subtle and unsettling legends, his images of yesterday designed to guard against undue folly today" [Hoyt W. Fuller, "The Raconteur," *Black World,* April 1967, 50]. Brown's poetry readings to the young were no less successful than his renderings of the extraordinary stories to which Fuller alluded.

4. As a consequence of such a judgment, editors of anthologies and professors of Negro literature apparently assumed that the only Brown poems worth reading were those which had appeared in previous anthologies. How else, after all, can one account for the same Sterling Brown poems in anthology after anthology? Perhaps a second printing of *Southern Road* would have militated against such a trend. Frederic Ramsey, Jr., distinguished folklorist and jazz authority, was employed at Harcourt, Brace and Company at the time the decision was made not to order a second printing of *Southern Road.* Ramsey "Protested the book's going out of print, and can remember the answer that came back from the head of the sales department: 'It wouldn't pay us.' Possibly not" [Frederic Ramsey, Jr., editor, "Sixteen Poems of Sterling A. Brown read by Sterling A. Brown," *Folkway Records,* album no. FL9794, 1973].

Southern Road constitutes slightly less than one-third of Sterling Brown's poetry. A few years following the publication of *Southern Road,* Brown submitted his second manuscript to Harcourt, Brace and Company, to be entitled *No Hiding Place;* it was rejected. The rejection of that manuscript, said to be on a level with *Southern Road,* remains something of a mystery. There is reason to believe, however, that more than possible sales considerations figured into the decision. *No Hiding Place* and *36 Poems 36 Years Later* are expected to be published soon. The appearance of these volumes, together with this reprint of *Southern Road,* should move Brown back to the center of Negro poetry—indeed, toward the center of American poetry, a position which he occupied shortly after the publication of *Southern Road.*

5. Alain Locke, "Sterling Brown: The New Negro Folk-Poet," Nancy Cunard, *Negro Anthology* (Wishart Co., 1934), p. 111.

6. *Ibid.,* p. 112.

7. *Ibid.,* p. 114.

8. *Ibid.,* p. 115.

9. Louis Untermeyer, "New Light from an Old Mine," *Opportunity,* August 1932, p. 250.

10. *Ibid.*

11. *Ibid.*

12. *Ibid.,* p. 251.

13. *The New Republic,* July 27, 1932, p. 297.

14. *The Nation,* July 13, 1932, p. 43. It should be noted that Sterling Brown has no objections to his poetry's being called dialect, providing it is understood that he rejects, through his poetry, the constricted definition earlier given to dialect by James Weldon Johnson—that is, that dialect has but two stops: humor and pathos. Brown has shown the remarkable resources of the language, demonstrating that dialect has as many stops as there are human emotions. Brown, in fact, has given us the first real look at the written language, in all its variety and richness, linked as it should be to the real-life people who created it. Thus, if the term *dialect* is to be used at all in describing much of the work of Brown, it should be understood that his is a wholly new conception.

15. William Rose Benét, "A New Negro Poet," *The Saturday Review of Literature,* May 14, 1932, p. 732.

16. *Ibid.*

17. "A Notable New Book of Negro Poetry," *The New York Times Book Review,* May 15, 1932.

18. *Ibid.,* p. 13.

19. See Sterling Nelson Brown, *My Own Life* (Hamilton, 1924).

20. Stephen Henderson's *Understanding the New Black Poetry* (Morrow, 1973) contains "Cabaret." Henderson's criticism of Brown in *Black World* was perhaps the first sensitive and scholarly treatment of Brown's poetry by a Negro since the generation of Locke and James Weldon Johnson. In providing a level of criticism worthy of the seriousness of Brown's art, Jean Wagner, in *Black Poetry* (University of Illinois Press, 1973), joins Henderson. For Henderson's essay on Brown's poetry, see "A Strong Man Called Sterling Brown," *Black World,* September 1970.

21. See Nathan Irvin Huggins, *Harlem Renaissance* (Oxford University Press, 1971), pp. 78, 221, 222, 225–227, 228. But Brown has challenged the very conception that a "Harlem Renaissance" took place: "The New Negro is not to me a group of writers centered in Harlem during the second half of the twenties. Most of the writers were not Harlemites; much of the best writing was not about Harlem, which was the show-window, the cashier's till, but no more Negro America than New York is America" [Sterling A. Brown, "The New Negro in Literature, 1925–1955," in *The New Negro Thirty Years Afterwards,* edited by Rayford Logan et al. (Washington: Howard University Press, 1955), p. 57].

22. See Lionel Trilling's introduction to George Orwell, *Homage to Catalonia* (New York: Harcourt, Brace and World, Inc., A Harvest Book, 1952), p. viii. Daisy Turnbull Brown, the wife of Sterling Brown, has helped him live this vision—in his poetry as in life. She is introduced in several poems in the last section of the volume, including "Thoughts of Death":

> *Death will come to you, I think,*
> *Like an old shrewd gardener*
> *Culling his rarest blossom . . .*

and the magical "Mill Mountain"

> *. . . We have learned tonight*
> *That there are havens from all desperate seas,*
> *And every ruthless war rounds into peace.*
> *It seems to me that Love can be that peace . . .*

Introduction
to the First Edition

In any inquiry regarding the important developments that have taken place in American Negro life within the past decade, I should at once cite the degree of ascendancy reached by the Negro artist, especially the Negro writer, as one of the most significant and vital.

The record of the Negro's efforts in literature goes back a long way, covering a period of more than a century and a half, but it is only within the past ten years that America as a whole has been made consciously aware of the Negro as a literary artist. It is only within that brief time that Negro writers have ceased to be regarded as isolated cases of exceptional, perhaps accidental ability, and have gained group recognition. It is only within these few years that the arbiters of American letters have begun to assay the work of these writers by the general literary standards and accord it such appraisal as it might merit.

This more sensitive awareness on the part of America as a whole to the existence and efforts of Negro writers, this wider recognition and less conditional appreciation of their work began with the rise of what is termed the "Younger Group." This group has consisted of about twenty-five writers doing acceptable work; and from them have risen some twelve who have gained more or less of national recognition. Among the writers of poetry in this smaller group the five names most outstanding are: Claude McKay, Jean Toomer, Countee Cullen, Langston Hughes and Sterling Brown. (I am naming them in the order of their emergence.) These "younger" poets are, naturally, younger in years than their predecessors, but the thing of greater consequence is that they are on the whole newer in their response to what still remains the principal motive of poetry written by Negroes—"race." In their approach to "race" they are less direct and obvious, less didactic or imploratory; and, too, they are less regardful of the approval or disapprobation of their white environment.

Sterling A. Brown is one of this group and therefore has been instrumental in bringing about the more propitious era in which the Negro artist now finds himself, and in doing that he has achieved a place in the list of young American poets. Mr. Brown's work is not only fine, it is also unique. He began writing just after the Negro poets had generally discarded conventionalized dialect, with its minstrel traditions of Negro life (traditions that had but slight relation, often no relation at all, to *actual* Negro life) with its artificial and false sentiment, its exaggerated geniality and optimism. He infused his poetry with genuine characteristic flavor by adopting as his medium the common, racy, living speech of the Negro in certain phases of *real* life. For his raw material he dug down into the deep mine of Negro folk poetry. He found the unfailing sources from which sprang the Negro folk epics and ballads such as "Stagolee," "John Henry," "Casey Jones," "Long Gone John" and others.

But, as I said in commenting on his work in *The Book of American Negro Poetry:* he has made more than mere transcriptions of folk poetry, and he has done more than bring to it mere artistry; he has deepened its meanings and multiplied its implications. He has actually absorbed the spirit of his material, made it his own; and without diluting its primitive frankness and raciness, truly re-expressed it with artistry and magnified power. In a word, he has taken this raw material and worked it into original and authentic poetry. In such poems as "Odyssey of Big Boy" and "Long Gone" he makes us feel the urge that drives the Negro wandering worker from place to place, from job to job, from woman to woman. There is that not much known characteristic, Negro stoicism, in "Memphis Blues" and there is Negro stoicism and black tragedy, too, in "Southern Road." Through the "Slim Greer" series he gives free play to a delicious ironical humor that is genuinely Negro. Many of these poems admit of no classification or brand, as, for example, the gorgeous "Sporting Beasley." True, this poem is Negro, but, intrinsically, it is Sterling-Brownian. In such poems as "Slim Greer," "Mister Samuel and Sam" and "Sporting Beasley" Mr. Brown discloses the possession of a quality that could to advantage be more common among Negro poets—the ability to laugh, to laugh at white folks as well as at black folks.

Mr. Brown has included in this volume some excellent poems written in literary English and form. I feel, however, it is in his poems whose sources are the folk life that he makes, beyond question, a distinctive contribution to American Poetry.

JAMES WELDON JOHNSON

Fisk University
Nashville, Tennessee

Part One

ROAD SO ROCKY

Road may be rocky,
Won't be rocky long. . . .
SPIRITUAL

for Anne Spencer

Odyssey of Big Boy

Lemme be wid Casey Jones,
   Lemme be wid Stagolee,
Lemme be wid such like men
   When Death takes hol' on me,
     When Death takes hol' on me. . . .

Done skinned as a boy in Kentucky hills,
   Druv steel dere as a man,
Done stripped tobacco in Virginia fiel's
   Alongst de River Dan,
     Alongst de River Dan;

Done mined de coal in West Virginia,
   Liked dat job jes' fine,
Till a load o' slate curved roun' my head,
   Won't work in no mo' mine,
     Won't work in no mo' mine;

Done shocked de corn in Marylan',
   In Georgia done cut cane,
Done planted rice in South Caline,
   But won't do dat again,
     Do dat no mo' again.

Been roustabout in Memphis,
   Dockhand in Baltimore,
Done smashed up freight on Norfolk wharves,
   A fust class stevedore,
     A fust class stevedore. . . .

Done slung hash yonder in de North
   On de ole Fall River Line,
Done busted suds in li'l New York,
   Which ain't no work o' mine—
     Lawd, ain't no work o' mine.

Done worked and loafed on such like jobs,
   Seen what dey is to see,
Done had my time wid a pint on my hip

An' a sweet gal on my knee,
    Sweet mommer on my knee:

Had stovepipe blond in Macon,
    Yaller gal in Marylan',
In Richmond had a choklit brown,
    Called me huh monkey man—
        Huh big fool monkey man.

Had two fair browns in Arkansaw
    And three in Tennessee,
Had Creole gal in New Orleans,
    Sho Gawd did two time me—
        Lawd two time, fo' time me—

But best gal what I evah had
    Done put it over dem,
A gal in Southwest Washington
    At Four'n half and M—
        Four'n half and M. . . .

Done took my livin' as it came,
    Done grabbed my joy, done risked my life;
Train done caught me on de trestle,
    Man done caught me wid his wife,
        His doggone purty wife. . . .

I done had my women,
    i done had my fun;
Cain't do much complainin'
    When my jag is done,
        Lawd, Lawd, my jag is done.

An' all dat Big Boy axes
    When time comes fo' to go,
Lemme be wid John Henry, steel drivin' man,
    Lemme be wid old Jazzbo,
        Lemme be wid ole Jazzbo. . . .

Long Gone

I laks yo' kin' of lovin',
　　Ain't never caught you wrong,
But it jes' ain' nachal
　　Fo' to stay here long;

It jes' ain' nachal
　　Fo' a railroad man,
With a itch fo' travelin'
　　He cain't understan'. . . .

I looks at de rails,
　　An' I looks at de ties,
An' I hears an ole freight
　　Puffin' up de rise,

An' at nights on my pallet,
　　When all is still,
I listens fo' de empties
　　Bumpin' up de hill;

When I oughta be quiet,
　　I is got a itch
Fo' to hear de whistle blow
　　Fo' de crossin' or de switch,

An' I knows de time's a-nearin'
　　When I got to ride,
Though it's homelike and happy
　　At yo' side.

You is done all you could do
　　To make me stay;
'Tain't no fault of yours I'se leavin'—
　　I'se jes dataway.

I is got to see some people
　　I ain't never seen,
Gotta highball thu some country
　　Whah I never been.

I don't know which way I'm travelin'—
   Far or near,
All I knows fo' certain is
   I cain't stay here.

Ain't no call at all, sweet woman,
   Fo' to carry on—
Jes' my name and jes' my habit
   To be Long Gone. . . .

Maumee Ruth

Might as well bury her
   And bury her deep,
Might as well put her
   Where she can sleep.

Might as well lay her
   Out in her shiny black;
And for the love of God
   Not wish her back.

Maum Sal may miss her—
   Maum Sal, she only—
With no one now to scoff,
   Sal may be lonely. . . .

Nobody else there is
   Who will be caring
How rocky was the road
   For her wayfaring;

Nobody be heeding in
   Cabin, or town,
That she is lying here
   In her best gown.

Boy that she suckled—
   How should he know,
Hiding in city holes,
   Sniffing the 'snow'?

And how should the news
   Pierce Harlem's din,
To reach her baby gal,
   Sodden with gin?

To cut her withered heart
   They cannot come again,
Preach her the lies about
   Jordan, and then

Might as well drop her
  Deep in the ground,
Might as well pray for her,
  That she sleep sound. . . .

When de Saints Go Ma'ching Home

(To Big Boy Davis, Friend.
In Memories of Days Before He Was
Chased Out of Town for Vagrancy.)

I

He'd play, after the bawdy songs and blues,
After the weary plaints
Of "Trouble, Trouble deep down in muh soul,"
Always one song in which he'd lose the rôle
Of entertainer to the boys. He'd say,
"My mother's favorite." And we knew
That what was coming was his chant of saints,
"When de saints go ma'chin' home. . . ."
And that would end his concert for the day.

Carefully as an old maid over needlework,
Oh, as some black deacon, over his Bible, lovingly,
He'd tune up specially for this. There'd be
No chatter now, no patting of the feet.
After a few slow chords, knelling and sweet—
Oh when de saints go ma'chin' home,
Oh when de sayaints goa ma'chin' home. . . .
He would forget
The quieted bunch, his dimming cigarette
Stuck into a splintered edge of the guitar;
Sorrow deep hidden in his voice, a far
And soft light in his strange brown eyes;
Alone with his masterchords, his memories. . . .
  Lawd I wanna be one in nummer
  When de saints go ma'chin' home.
Deep the bass would rumble while the treble scattered high,
For all the world like heavy feet a-trompin' toward the sky,
With shrill-voiced women getting 'happy'
All to celestial tunes.
The chap's few speeches helped me understand
The reason why he gazed so fixedly
Upon the burnished strings.

For he would see
A gorgeous procession to 'de Beulah Land,'—
Of saints—his friends—*"a-climbin' fo' deir wings."*
Oh when de saints go ma'chin' home. . . .
Lawd I wanna be one o' dat nummer
When de saints goa ma'chin' home. . . .

II

There'd be—so ran his dream:
> "Ole Deacon Zachary
> With de asthmy in his chest,
> A-puffin' an' a-wheezin'
> Up de golden stair;
> Wid de badges of his lodges
> Strung acrost his heavin' breast
> An' de hoggrease jes' shinin'
> In his coal black hair. . . .

> "An' ole Sis Joe
> In huh big straw hat,
> An' huh wrapper flappin',
> Flappin' in de heavenly win',
> An' huh thin-soled easy walkers
> Goin' pitty pitty pat,—
> Lawd she'd have to ease her corns
> When she got in!"

Oh when de saints go ma'chin' home.
> "Ole Elder Peter Johnson
> Wid his corncob jes' a-puffin',
> An' de smoke a-rollin'
> Lak stormclouds out behin';
> Crossin' de cloud mountains
> Widout slowin' up fo' nuffin,
> Steamin' up de grade
> Lak Wes' bound No. 9.

> "An' de little brown-skinned chillen
> Wid deir skinny legs a-dancin',
> Jes' a-kickin' up ridic'lous
> To de heavenly band;

Lookin' at de Great Drum Major
On a white hoss jes' a-prancin',
Wid a gold and silver drumstick
A-waggin' in his han'."
Oh when de sun refuse to shine
Oh when de mo-on goes down
                In Blood
"Ole Maumee Annie
Wid huh washin' done,
An' huh las' piece o' laundry
In de renchin' tub,
A wavin' sof' pink han's
To de much obligin' sun,
An' her feet a-moverin' now
To a swif' rub-a-dub;

"An' old Grampa Eli
Wid his wrinkled old haid,
A-puzzlin' over summut
He ain' understood,
Intendin' to ask Peter
Pervidin' he ain't skyaid,
'Jes' what mought be de meanin'
Of de moon in blood?' . . ."
When de saints go ma'chin' home. . . .

III

"Whuffolks," he dreams, *"will have to stay outside*
Being so onery." But what is he to do
With that red brakeman who once let him ride
An empty going home? Or with that kind-faced man
Who paid his songs with board and drink and bed?
Or with the Yankee Cap'n who left a leg
At Vicksburg? *Mought be a place, he said,*
Mought be another mansion fo' white saints,
A smaller one than his'n . . . not so gran'.
As fo' the rest . . . oh let 'em howl and beg.
Hell would be good enough—if big enough—
Widout no shade trees, lawd, widout no rain.
Whuffolks sho' to bring nigger out behin',
Excep'—"when de saints go ma'chin' home."

28

IV

Sportin' Legs would not be there—nor lucky Sam,
Nor Smitty, nor Hambone, nor Hardrock Gene,
An' not too many guzzlin', cuttin' shines,
Nor bootleggers to keep his pockets clean.
An' Sophie wid de sof' smile on her face,
Her foolin' voice, her strappin' body, brown
Lak coffee doused wid milk—she had been good
To him, wid lovin', money and wid food.—
But saints and heaven didn't seem to fit
Jes' right wid Sophy's Beauty—nary bit—
She mought stir trouble, somehow, in dat peaceful place
Mought be some dressed-up dudes in dat fair town.

V

Ise got a dear ole mudder,
She is in hebben I know—
He sees:
    Mammy,
    Li'l mammy—wrinkled face,
    Her brown eyes, quick to tears—to joy—
    With such happy pride in her
    Guitar-plunkin' boy.
    Oh kain't I be one in nummer?

    Mammy
    With deep religion defeating the grief
    Life piled so closely about her,
    Ise so glad trouble doan last alway,
    And her dogged belief
    That some fine day
    She'd go a-ma'chin'
    When de saints go ma'chin' home.

He sees her ma'chin' home, ma'chin' along,
Her perky joy shining in her furrowed face,
Her weak and quavering voice singing her song—
The best chair set apart for her worn out body
In that restful place. . . .
    I pray to de Lawd I'll meet her
    When de saints go ma'chin' home.

VI

He'd shuffle off from us, always, at that,—
His face a brown study beneath his torn brimmed hat,
His broad shoulders slouching, his old box strung
Around his neck;—he'd go where we
Never could follow him—to Sophie probably,
Or to his dances in old Tinbridge flat.

Dark of the Moon

Plant a fence post
On de dark uh de moon,
Locust, oak, hickory,
Any uh dose
Yuh plant it fo' nothin',
Yuh plant it fo' rottin',
Is a ole head's sayin',
An' a ole head knows.

Daniel was likely
An' Daniel was handsome,
Quick at his fingers,
Promisin' lad;
Joy of his hard-handed
Bent-over mammy,
Hope of his slow-drawlin'
Upstandin' dad.

Mammy died early;
Dad took to Daniel,
All dat he had to
Keep his heart warm;
Nothin' but Daniel,
Smart boy an' handsome,
To drive off his mopin',
To keep him his farm.

Dan got a hongry
Longin' fo' sweetnen talk,
His travelin' feet
Allus itchin' to go
Down to de settlement,
Down to de fancy gals,
Where he never found out
What his dad wanted so.

But Dan was a smart 'un,
Big, flashy rascal,
Dan got to be
De sweet man uh town;

Sweet man fo' hussies,
Badman fo' poolrooms,
Was drunk when dey dropped
His dad in de groun'.

Ole folks who passed by
De farm up fo' auction,
Knew why his hard dad
Wore out so soon;
Shook dey heads solemn,
Thinking uh Daniel
"Must uh been bo'n
On de dark uh de moon."

Seeking Religion

Lulu walked forlornly in late April twilight,
Lulu sought religion, long urged by Parson Jones,
Lulu sought the pinewoods, sought the dusky graveyard,
Fought her fears and sat among the ghostlike stones.

Waiting for her visions, but not so very eager,
Lulu sat still with a crescent moon above,
Lulu dreamt dreams a creaky-jointed parson
Hadn't so much as warned her of.

Jim found Lulu sitting in the shadow,
Lulu was sobbing, her head upon her knees;
Jim spoke to Lulu, and realized her visions,
And scared off the strange things lurking in the trees.

Jim sought Lulu when harrowing was over,
The slim moon up; and with a convert's joy
Lulu sought religion in thick deep-shadowed pinewoods,
Lulu found religion in a chubby baby boy.

Georgie Grimes

Georgie Grimes, with a red suitcase,
  Sloshes onward through the rain,
Georgie Grimes, with a fear behind him,
  Will not come back again.

Georgie remembers hot words, lies,
  The knife, and a pool of blood,
And suddenly her staring eyes,
  With their light gone out for good.

Georgie mutters over and over,
  Stumbling through the soggy clay,
"No livin' woman got de right
  To do no man dat way."

Scotty Has His Say

Whuh folks, whuh folks; don' wuk muh brown too hahd!

    'Cause Ise crazy 'bout muh woman,
    An' ef yuh treats huh mean,
    I gonna sprinkle goofy dus'
    In yo' soup tureen.

Whuh folks, whuh folks; don' wuk muh brown too hahd!
Muh brown what's tendin' chillen in yo' big backyahd.

    Oh, dat gal is young an' tender,
    So jes' don' mistreat huh please,
    Or I'll put a sprig of pisen ivy
    In yo' B.V.D.'s.

    I got me a Blackcat's wishbone,
    Got some Blackcat's ankle dus',
    An' yuh crackers better watch out
    Ef I sees yo' carcass fus'—

Whuh folks, whuh folks; don' wuk muh brown too hahd!
Muh brown what's wringin' chicken necks in yo' backyahd.

    'Cause muh brown an' me, we'se champeens
    At de St. Luke's Hall;
    An' yo' cookin' an' yo' washin'
    Jes' ain't in it, not at all,

    Wid de way we does de Chahlston,
    De Black Bottom an' cake walkin',
    Steppin' on de puppies' tail;
    Whuh folks, ain' no need in talkin',—

    You is got muh purty brownskin
    In yo' kitchen an' yo' yahd,
    Lemme tell yuh rebs one sho thing
    Doncha wuk muh brown too hahd—

Whuh folks, whuh folks; don' wuk muh brown too hahd!
Who's practisin' de Chahlston in yo' big backyahd.

Ruminations of Luke Johnson

I got me a question
Puzzlin' my brain,
But I'm too polite
An' I ain't gonna ask it;
But evah weekday mo'nin',
I see Mandy Jane
Trompin' to huh wuk
Wid a great big basket.

In de early mo'nin',
She swings it moughty easy,
An' 'pears to me at such times
It ain't no awful load;
But, ailus in de evenin'
A smell of somethin' greasy
Sneaks fum out de cover,
An' puhfumes up de road.

Den de basket seems a burden
Fo' even Mandy Jane;
But she doan puhmit no nigger
Fo' to he'p huh out;
She picks all de darkest
Places in de lane,
Where de hongry hounds sniff
An' foller huh about. . . .

Well, tain't my business noway,
An' I ain' near fo'gotten
De lady what she wuks fo',
An' how she got huh jack;
De money dat *she* live on
Come from niggers pickin' cotton,
Ebbery dollar dat she squander
Nearly bust a nigger's back.

So I'm glad dat in de evenin's
Mandy Jane seems extra happy,
An' de lady at de big house
Got no kick at all, I say;—

Cause what huh "dear grandfawthaw"
Took from Mandy Jane's grandpappy—
Ain' no basket in de worl'
What kin tote all dat away. . . .

Virginia Portrait

Winter is settling on the place; the sedge
Is dry and lifeless and the woods stand bare.
The late autumnal flowers, nipped by frost,
Break from the sear stalks in the trim, neat garden,
And fall unheeded on the bleak, brown earth.

The winter of her year has come to her,
This wizened woman, spare of frame, but great
Of heart, erect, and undefeated yet.

Grief has been hers, before this wintry time.
Death has paid calls, unmannered, uninvited;
Low mounds have swollen in the fenced off corner,
Over brown children, marked by white-washed stones.
She has seen hopes that promised a fine harvest
Burnt by the drought; or bitten by the hoarfrost;
Or washed up and drowned out by unlooked for rains.
And as a warning blast of her own winter,
Death, the harsh overseer, shouted to her man,
Who answering slowly went over the hill.

She, puffing on a jagged slow-burning pipe,
By the low hearthfire, knows her winter now.
But she has strength and steadfast hardihood.
Deep-rooted is she, even as the oaks,
Hardy as perennials about her door.
The circle of the seasons brings no fear,
"Folks all gits used to what dey sees so often";
And she has helps that throng her glowing fire
Mixed with the smoke hugging her grizzled head:

Warm friends, the love of her full-blooded spouse,
Quiet companionship as age crept on him,
Laughter of babies, and their shrewd, sane raising;
These simple joys, not poor to her at all;
The sight of smokeclouds pouring from the flue;
Her stalwart son deep busied with "book larnin',"
After the weary fields; the kettle's purr
In duet with the sleek and pampered mouser;

Twanging of dominickers; lowing of Betsey;
Old folksongs chanted underneath the stars. . . .

Even when winter settles on her heart,
She keeps a wonted, quiet nonchalance,
A courtly dignity of speech and carriage,
Unlooked for in these distant rural ways.

She has found faith sufficient for her grief,
The song of earth for bearing heavy years,
She with slow speech, and spurts of heartfelt laughter,
Illiterate, and somehow very wise.

She has been happy, and her heart is grateful.
Now she looks out, and forecasts unperturbed
Her following slowly over the lonesome hill,
Her *'layin' down her burdens, bye and bye.'*

Old Man Buzzard

Old Man Buzzard
Wid his bal' head,
Flopped in de fiel'
An' eyed young Fred,
Clacked his beak, an'
Den he said:

"Youse got a plump gal,
Roun' and strong,
Promise she'll love yuh,
Woan go wrong,
Lemme tell yuh, big boy,
Cain't last long.

"Buddy on de next farm,
Good ole frien',
Got no dimes
But what he'll len',
Friendship fine,
But friendship en'—

"Yuh gits good vittels
Likes yo' co'n,
Ain' been sick
Sence yuh was bawn,
All sich good luck
Soon be gone.

"Death comes a-orderin'
Folks aroun',
Got blacksnake whip
Bring yuh down—
Yo' frien' cain't help you
Nor yo' brown—"

Fred look up
When he hear dis trash,
Grin crack his mouth
An' de lightnin' flash,

Thoe back his head
An' de thunder crash:

"Whoever sent yuh
Tell him, say,
Fred leave frettin'
Fo' nother day;
Mister Bal'head Buzzard
Git away!

"Doan give a damn
Ef de good things go,
Game rooster yit,
Still kin crow,
Somp'n in my heart here
Makes me so.

"In roas'n ear time
A man eats co'n,
Dough he knows in winter
Co'n's all gone,
Worry's no good
To whet teeth on.

"No need in frettin'
Case good times go,
Things as dey happen
Jes' is so;
Nothin' las' always
Farz I know. . . ."

Johnny Thomas

Dey sent John Thomas
To a one-room school;
Teacher threw him out
For a consarned fool.

His pappy got drunk,—
Beat de boy good,
Lashed his back
Till it spouted blood.

He took up gamblin',
Took up pool,
A better business that
For a consarned fool.

He got a 'fancy woman'
Took his every dime,
Kept Johnny gamblin'
All de time.

De jack run low
De gal run out
Johnny didn't know
What 'twas all about.

Asked de fancy woman
"Come on back,"
Fancy woman tell him,
"Git de Jack."

Johnny was a tadpole,
Sheriff was a eel,
Caught him jes' as soon
As he started to steal.

Put him on de chain gang,
Handled him cruel,
Jes' de sort of treatment
For a consarned fool.

Guard lashed Johnny
An awful lick,
Johnny split his head
Wid a muddy pick.

Dey haltered Johnny Thomas
Like a cussed mule,
Dey hung Johnny Thomas
For a consarned fool.

Dropped him in de hole
Threw de slack lime on,
Oughta had mo' sense
Dan to evah git born.

Frankie and Johnny

Oh Frankie and Johnny were lovers
Oh Lordy how they did love!
OLD BALLAD

Frankie was a halfwit, Johnny was a nigger,
   Frankie liked to pain poor creatures as a little 'un,
Kept a crazy love of torment when she got bigger,
   Johnny had to slave it and never had much fun.

Frankie liked to pull wings off of living butterflies,
   Frankie liked to cut long angleworms in half,
Frankie liked to whip curs and listen to their drawn out cries,
   Frankie liked to shy stones at the brindle calf.

Frankie took her pappy's lunch week-days to the sawmill,
   Her pappy, red-faced cracker, with a cracker's thirst,
Beat her skinny body and reviled the hateful imbecile,
   She screamed at every blow he struck, but tittered when he curst.

Frankie had to cut through Johnny's field of sugar corn
   Used to wave at Johnny, who didn't *'pay no min'* —
Had had to work like fifty from the day that he was born,
   And wan't no cracker hussy gonna put his work behind—.

But everyday Frankie swung along the cornfield lane,
   And one day Johnny helped her partly through the wood,
Once he had dropped his plow lines, he dropped them many times again—
   Though his mother didn't know it, else she'd have whipped him good.

Frankie and Johnny were lovers; oh Lordy how they did love!
   But one day Frankie's pappy by a big log laid him low,
To find out what his crazy Frankie had been speaking of;
   He found that what his gal had muttered was exactly so.

Frankie, she was spindly limbed with corn silk on her crazy head,
   Johnny was a nigger, who never had much fun—
They swung up Johnny on a tree, and filled his swinging hide with lead,
   And Frankie yowled hilariously when the thing was done.

Sam Smiley

I

The whites had taught him how to rip
   A Nordic belly with a thrust
Of bayonet, had taught him how
   To transmute Nordic flesh to dust.

And a surprising fact had made
   Belated impress on his mind:
That shrapnel bursts and poison gas
   Were inexplicably color blind.

He picked up, from the difficult
   But striking lessons of the war,
Some truths that he could not forget,
   Though inconceivable before.

And through the lengthy vigils, stuck
   In never-drying stinking mud,
He was held up by dreams of one
   Chockfull of laughter, hot of blood.

II

On the return Sam Smiley cheered
   The dirty steerage with his dance,
Hot-stepping boy! Soon he would see
   The girl who beat all girls in France.

He stopped buckdancing when he reached
   The shanties at his journey's end;
He found his sweetheart in the jail,
   And took white lightning for his friend.

One night the woman whose full voice
   Had chortled so, was put away
Into a narrow gaping hole;
   Sam sat beside till break of day.

He had been told what man it was
  Whose child the girl had had to kill,
Who best knew why her laugh was dumb,
  Who best knew why her blood was still.

And he remembered France, and how
  A human life was dunghill cheap,
And so he sent a rich white man
  His woman's company to keep.

III

The mob was in fine fettle, yet
  The dogs were stupid-nosed, and day
Was far spent when the men drew round
  The scrawny woods where Smiley lay.

The oaken leaves drowsed prettily,
  The moon shone down benignly there;
And big Sam Smiley, King Buckdancer,
  Buckdanced on the midnight air.

To Sallie, Walking

Your vividness grants color where
   Great need is, in this dingy town,
   As you in pride of rose and brown
    Thread the dull thoroughfare.

Across the Southern sleepiness
   Flashes a something swiftly real:
   The unavoidable appeal
    Of your sharp loveliness.

And not as Cavalier scions, do
   These listless Southrons, furtive-eyed,
   Greet gracefully your proper pride,—
    But wonderstruck at you,

Regret awhile, that aliens
   They will remain, darkly allured
   By an inviolable, assured,
    Laughing indifference.

You pass, provocative, discreet,
   Serenely waving to his place,
   Each lover of your bronzen face,
    Your merry, flashing feet.

The impudence filling your eyes
   Will call down on your swarthy head
   The wildest prayers that men have prayed;
    Malignant prophecies.

But lovers' wrathful violence
   You will put by as lunacy,
   In Age's longdrawn mutterings see
    Cantankerous impotence.

Oh, as you walk, lithe, delicate,
   Parading in your rose-red dress,
   There is this much that I can guess:
    The labyrinthine Fate,—

The plotting of dire circumstance,
 Which intricate before you lies,
 Will be as nothing to your wise
  Inherent nonchalance.

Bessie

Who will know Bessie now of those who loved her;
   Who of her gawky pals could recognize
Bess in this woman, gaunt of flesh and painted,
   Despair deep bitten in her soft brown eyes?

Would the lads who walked with her in dusk-cooled byways
   Know Bessie now should they meet her again?
Would knowing men of Fifth St. think that Bessie ever
   Was happy-hearted, brave-eyed as she was then?

Bessie with her plaited hair, Bessie in her gingham,
   Bessie with her bird voice, and laughter like the sun,
Bess who left behind the stupid, stifling shanties,
   And took her to the cities to get her share of fun. . . .

Her mammy and her dad for whom she was a darling,
   Who talked of her at night, and dreamt dreams so—
They wouldn't know her now, even if they were knowing,
   And it's well for them they went just as soon as they did go.

Kentucky Blues

I'm Kentucky born,
Kentucky bred,
Gonna brag about Kentucky
Till I'm dead.

Thoroughbred horses,
Hansome, fas',
I ain't got nothin'
But a dam' jackass.

Women as purty
As Kingdom Come,
Ain't got no woman
'Cause I'm black and dumb.

Cornland good,
Tobacco land fine,
Can't raise nothin'
On dis hill o' mine.

Ain't got no woman,
Nor no Man O' War,
But dis nigger git
What he's hankering for—

De red licker's good,
An' it ain't too high,
Gonna brag about Kentucky
Till I die. . . .

Mister Samuel and Sam

Mister Samuel, he belong to Rotary,
Sam to de Sons of Rest;
Both wear red hats lak monkey men,
An' you cain't say which is de best.

Mister Samuel ride in a Cadillac,
Sam ride in a Tin Lizzie Fo'd;
Both spend their jack fo' gas an' oil,
An' both git stuck on de road.

Mister Samuel speak in de Chamber of Commerce,
Sam he speak in ch'uch;
Both of 'em talk for a mighty long time,
Widout sayin', Lawd knows, ve'y much.

Mister Samuel deal wid high finance,
Sam deal in a two-bit game;
Mister Samuel crashes, Sam goes broke,
But deys busted jes' de same.

Mister Samuel wife speak sof' an' low,
When dey gits in their weekly fight;
Sam catches a broomstick crost his rear,
An' both of 'em's henpecked right.

Mister Samuel drinks his Canadian Rye,
Sam drinks his bootleg gin;
Both gits as high as a Georgia pine,
And both calls de doctor in.

Mister Samuel die, an' de folks all know,
Sam die widout no noise;
De worl' go by in de same ol' way,
And dey's both of 'em po' los' boys. . . .

Southern Road

Swing dat hammer—hunh—
Steady, bo';
Swing dat hammer—hunh—
Steady, bo';
Ain't no rush, bebby,
Long ways to go.

Burner tore his—hunh—
Black heart away;
Burner tore his—hunh—
Black heart away;
Got me life, bebby,
An' a day.

Gal's on Fifth Street—hunh—
Son done gone;
Gal's on Fifth Street—hunh—
Son done gone;
Wife's in de ward, bebby,
Babe's not bo'n.

My ole man died—hunh—
Cussin' me;
My ole man died—hunh—
Cussin' me;
Ole lady rocks, bebby,
Huh misery.

Doubleshackled—hunh—
Guard behin';
Doubleshackled—hunh—
Guard behin';
Ball an' chain, bebby,
On my min'.

White man tells me—hunh—
Damn yo' soul;
White man tells me—hunh—
Damn yo' soul;

Got no need, bebby,
To be tole.

Chain gang nevah—hunh—
Let me go;
Chain gang nevah—hunh—
Let me go;
Po' los' boy, bebby,
Evahmo'. . . .

Sister Lou

Honey
When de man
Calls out de las' train
You're gonna ride,
Tell him howdy.

Gather up yo' basket
An' yo' knittin' an' yo' things,
An' go on up an' visit
Wid frien' Jesus fo' a spell.

Show Marfa
How to make yo' greengrape jellies,
An' give po' Lazarus
A passel of them Golden Biscuits.

Scald some meal
Fo' some rightdown good spoonbread
Fo' li'l box-plunkin' David.

An' sit aroun'
An' tell them Hebrew Chillen
All yo' stories. . . .

Honey
Don't be feared of them pearly gates,
Don't go 'round to de back,
No mo' dataway
Not evah no mo'.

Let Michael tote yo' burden
An' yo' pocketbook an' evahthing
'Cept yo' Bible,
While Gabriel blows somp'n
Solemn but loudsome
On dat horn of his'n.

Honey
Go straight on to de Big House,

An' speak to yo' God
Widout no fear an' tremblin'.

Then sit down
An' pass de time of day awhile.

Give a good talkin' to
To yo' favorite 'postle Peter,
An' rub the po' head
Of mixed-up Judas,
An' joke awhile wid Jonah.

Then, when you gits de chance,
Always rememberin' yo' raisin',
Let 'em know youse tired
Jest a mite tired.

Jesus will find yo' bed fo' you
Won't no servant evah bother wid yo' room.
Jesus will lead you
To a room wid windows
Openin' on cherry trees an' plum trees
Bloomin' everlastin'.

An' dat will be yours
Fo' keeps.

Den take yo' time. . . .
Honey, take yo' bressed time.

Strong Men

The young men keep coming on
The strong men keep coming on.
SANDBURG

They dragged you from homeland,
They chained you in coffles,
They huddled you spoon-fashion in filthy hatches,
They sold you to give a few gentlemen ease.

They broke you in like oxen,
They scourged you,
They branded you,
They made your women breeders,
They swelled your numbers with bastards. . . .
They taught you the religion they disgraced.

You sang:
    Keep a-inchin' along
    Lak a po' inch worm. . . .

You sang:
    Bye and bye
    I'm gonna lay down dis heaby load. . . .

You sang:
    Walk togedder, chillen,
    Dontcha git weary. . . .
      The strong men keep a-comin' on
      The strong men git stronger.

They point with pride to the roads you built for them,
They ride in comfort over the rails you laid for them.
They put hammers in your hands
And said—Drive so much before sundown.

You sang:
    Ain't no hammah
    In dis lan',

Strikes lak mine, bebby,
Strikes lak mine.

They cooped you in their kitchens,
They penned you in their factories,
They gave you the jobs that they were too good for,
They tried to guarantee happiness to themselves
By shunting dirt and misery to you.

You sang:
    Me an' muh baby gonna shine, shine
    Me an' muh baby gonna shine.
      The strong men keep a-comin' on
      The strong men git stronger. . . .

They bought off some of your leaders
You stumbled, as blind men will . . .
They coaxed you, unwontedly soft-voiced. . . .
You followed a way.
Then laughed as usual.

They heard the laugh and wondered;
Uncomfortable,
Unadmitting a deeper terror. . . .
      The strong men keep a-comin', on
      Gittin' stronger. . . .

What, from the slums
Where they have hemmed you,
What, from the tiny huts
They could not keep from you—
What reaches them
Making them ill at ease, fearful?
Today they shout prohibition at you
"Thou shalt not this"
"Thou shalt not that"
"Reserved for whites only"
You laugh.

One thing they cannot prohibit—
      The strong men . . . coming on

The strong men gittin' stronger.
Strong men. . . .
Stronger. . . .

Part Two

ON RESTLESS RIVER

O, de Mississippi River, so deep an' wide. . . .
(BLUES)

for Allison Davis

Memphis Blues

Nineveh, Tyre,
Babylon,
Not much lef'
Of either one.
All dese cities
Ashes and rust,
De win' sing sperrichals
Through deir dus' . . .
Was another Memphis
Mongst de olden days,
Done been destroyed
In many ways. . . .
Dis here Memphis
It may go;
Floods may drown it;
Tornado blow;
Mississippi wash it
Down to sea—
Like de other Memphis in
History.

II

Watcha gonna do when Memphis on fire,
    Memphis on fire, Mistah Preachin' Man?
Gonna pray to Jesus and nebber tire,
    Gonna pray to Jesus, loud as I can,
        Gonna pray to my Jesus, oh, my Lawd!

Watcha gonna do when de tall flames roar,
    Tall flames roar, Mistah Lovin' Man?
Gonna love my brownskin better'n before—
    Gonna love my baby lak a do right man,
        Gonna love my brown baby, oh, my Lawd!

Watcha gonna do when Memphis falls down,
    Memphis falls down, Mistah Music Man?
Gonna plunk on dat box as long as it soun',

Gonna plunk dat box fo' to beat de ban',
   Gonna tickle dem ivories, oh, my Lawd!

Watcha gonna do in de hurricane,
   In de hurricane, Mistah Workin' Man?
Gonna put dem buildings up again,
   Gonna put em up dis time to stan',
      Gonna push a wicked wheelbarrow, oh, my Lawd!

Watcha gonna do when Memphis near gone,
   Memphis near gone, Mistah Drinkin' Man?
Gonna grab a pint bottle of Mountain-Corn,
   Gonna keep de stopper in my han',
      Gonna get a mean jag on, oh, my Lawd!

Watcha gonna do when de flood roll fas',
   Flood roll fas', Mistah Gamblin' Man?
Gonna pick up my dice fo' one las' pass—
   Gonna fade my way to de lucky lan',
      Gonna throw my las' seven—oh, my Lawd!

III

Memphis go
By Flood or Flame;
Nigger won't worry
All de same—
Memphis go
Memphis come back,
Ain' no skin
Off de nigger's back.
All dese cities
Ashes, rust. . . .
De win' sing sperrichals
Through deir dus'.

Ma Rainey

I

When Ma Rainey
Comes to town,
Folks from anyplace
Miles aroun',
From Cape Girardeau,
Poplar Bluff,
Flocks in to hear
Ma do her stuff;
Comes flivverin' in,
Or ridin' mules,
Or packed in trains,
Picknickin' fools. . . .
That's what it's like,
Fo' miles on down,
To New Orleans delta
An' Mobile town,
When Ma hits
Anywheres aroun'.

II

Dey comes to hear Ma Rainey from de little river settlements,
From blackbottom cornrows and from lumber camps;
Dey stumble in de hall, jes a-laughin' an' a-cacklin',
Cheerin' lak roarin' water, lak wind in river swamps.

An' some jokers keeps deir laughs a-goin' in de crowded aisles,
An' some folks sits dere waitin' wid deir aches an' miseries,
Till Ma comes out before dem, a-smilin' gold-toofed smiles
An' Long Boy ripples minors on de black an' yellow keys.

III

O Ma Rainey,
Sing yo' song;
Now you's back
Whah you belong,
Git way inside us,
Keep us strong. . . .

O Ma Rainey,
Li'l an' low;
Sing us 'bout de hard luck
Roun' our do';
Sing us 'bout de lonesome road
We mus' go. . . .

IV

I talked to a fellow, an' the fellow say,
"She jes' catch hold of us, somekindaway.
She sang Backwater Blues one day:

> 'It rained fo' days an' de skies was dark as night,
> Trouble taken place in de lowlands at night.

> 'Thundered an' lightened an' the storm begin to roll
> Thousan's of people ain't got no place to go.

> 'Den I went an' stood upon some high ol' lonesome hill,
> An' looked down on the place where I used to live.'

An' den de folks, dey natchally bowed dey heads an' cried,
Bowed dey heavy heads, shet dey moufs up tight an' cried,
An' Ma lef' de stage, an' followed some de folks outside."

Dere wasn't much more de fellow say:
She jes' gits hold of us dataway.

Old King Cotton

Ole King Cotton,
Ole Man Cotton,
Keeps us slavin'
Till we'se dead an' rotten.

Bosses us 'roun'
In his ornery way,
"Cotton needs pickin'!"
De Hell he say. . . .

Starves us wid bumper crops,
Starves us wid po',
Chains de lean wolf
At our do'.

Tiahed uh co'n pone,
Pork an' greens,
Fat back an' sorghum,
An' dried up beans.

Buy one rusty mule
To git ahead—
We stays in debt
Until we'se dead;

Ef flood don't git us
It's de damn bo' weevil
Crap grass in de drought,
Or somp'n else evil;

Ef we gits de bales
When de hard luck's gone,
Bill at de commissary
Goes right on.

Some planters goes broke,
An' some gits well,
But dey sits on deir bottoms
Feelin' swell;

An' us in de crap grass
Catchin' hell.

Cotton, cotton,
All we know;
Plant cotton, hoe it,
Baig it to grow;
What good it do to us
Gawd only know!

Children of the Mississippi

These know fear; for all their singing
As the moon thrust her tip above dark woods,
Tuning their voices to the summer night,
These folk knew even then the hints of fear.
For all their loafing on the levee,
Unperturbedly spendthrift of time,
Greeting the big boat swinging the curve
"Do it, Mister Pilot! Do it, Big Boy!"
Beneath their dark laughter
Roaring like a flood roars, swung into a spillway,
There rolled even then a strong undertow
Of fear.

Now, intimately
These folk know fear.
They have seen
Blackwater creeping, slow-footed Fate,
Implacably, unceasingly
Over their bottomlands, over their cornshocks,
Past highwater marks, past wildest conjecture,
Black water creeping before their eyes,
Rolling while they toss in startled half sleep.

> *De Lord tole Norah*
> *Dat de flood was due,*
> *Norah listened to de Lord*
> *An' got his stock on board,*
> *Wish dat de Lord*
> *Had tole us too.*

These folk know grief.
They have seen
Black water gurgling, lapping, roaring,
Take their lives' earnings, roll off their paltry
Fixtures of home, things as dear as old hearthgods.
These have known death
Surprising, rapacious of cattle, of children,
Creeping with the black water
Secretly, unceasingly.

> *Death pick out new ways*
> *Now fo' to come to us,*
> *Black water creepin'*
> *While folks is sleepin',*
> *Death on de black water*
> *Ugly an' treacherous.*

These, for all their vaunted faith, know doubt.
These know no Ararat;
No arc of promise bedecking blue skies;
No dove, betokening calm;
No fondled favor towards new beginnings.
These know
Promise of baked lands, burnt as in brickkilns,
Cracked uglily, crinkled crust at the seedtime,
Rotten with stench, watched over by vultures.
Promise of winter, bleak and unpitying,
No buoyant hoping now, only dank memories
Bitter as the waters, bracken as the waters,
Black and unceasing as hostile waters.

> *Winter a-comin'*
> *Leaner dan ever,*
> *What we done done to you*
> *Makes you do lak you do?*
> *How we done harmed you*
> *Black-hearted river?*

These folk know fear, now, as a bosom crony;
Children, stepchildren
Of the Mississippi. . . .

New St. Louis Blues

MARKET STREET WOMAN

Market Street woman is known fuh to have dark days,
Market Street woman noted fuh to have dark days,
Life do her dirty in a hundred onery ways.

Let her hang out de window and watch de busy worl' go pas',
Hang her head out de window and watch de careless worl' go pas',
Maybe some good luck will come down Market Street at las'.

Put paint on her lips, purple powder on her choklit face,
Paint on her lips, purple powder on her choklit face,
Take mo' dan paint to change de luck of dis dam place.

Gettin' old and ugly, an' de sparks done lef' her eye,
Old an' ugly an' de fire's out in her eye,
De men may see her, but de men keeps passin' by—

Market Street woman have her hard times, oh my Lawd,
Market Street woman have her hard times, oh my Lawd,
Let her git what she can git, 'fo dey lays her on de coolin' board.

TORNADO BLUES

Black wind come a-speedin' down de river from de Kansas plains,
Black wind come a-speedin' down de river from de Kansas plains,
Black wind come a-roarin' like a flock of giant aeroplanes—

Destruction was a-drivin' it and close behind was Fear,
Destruction was a-drivin' it and hand in hand with Fear,
Grinnin' Death and skinny Sorrow was a-bringin' up de rear.

Dey got some ofays, but dey mostly got de Jews an' us,
Got some ofays, but mostly got de Jews an' us,
Many po' boys castle done settled to a heap o' dus'.

Newcomers dodge de mansions, and knocked on de po' folks' do',
Dodged most of the mansions, and knocked down de po' folks' do',
Never know us po' folks so popular befo'—

Foun' de moggidge unpaid, foun' de insurance long past due,
Moggidge unpaid, de insurance very long past due,
All de homes we wukked so hard for goes back to de Fay and Jew.

De Black wind evil, done done its dirty work an' gone,
Black wind evil, done done its dirty work an' gone,
Lawd help de folks what de wind ain't had no mercy on.

LOW DOWN

So low down bummin' cut plug from de passers by,
So low down bummin' cut plug from de passers by,
When a man bum tobacco ain't much lef' to do but die. . . .

Bone's gittin' brittle, an' my brain won't low no rest,
Bone's gittin' brittle, an' my brain won't let me rest,
Death drivin' rivets overtime in my scooped out chest.

Woman done quit me, my boy lies fast in jail,
Woman done quit me, pa'dner lies fast in jail,
Kin bum tobacco but I cain't bum de jack for bail.

Church don't help me, 'cause I ain't got no Sunday clothes,
Church don't help me, got no show off Sunday clothes,
Preachers and deacons, don't look to get no help from those.

Wouldn't mind dyin' but I ain't got de jack fo' toll,
Wouldn't mind dyin' but I'd have to bum de jack fo' toll,
Some dirty joker done put a jinx on my po' soul.

Dice are loaded, an' de deck's all marked to hell,
Dice are loaded, de deck's all marked to hell,
Whoever runs dis gamble sholy runs it well.

Foreclosure

Father Missouri takes his own.
These are the fields he loaned them,
Out of heart's fullness, gratuitously;
Here are the banks he built up for his children,
Here are the fields, rich fertile silt.

Father Missouri, in his dotage
Whimsical and drunkenly turbulent,
Cuts away the banks, steals away the loam,
Washes the ground from under wire fences,
Leaves fenceposts grotesquely dangling in the air;
And with doddering steps approaches the shanties.

Father Missouri, far too old to be so evil.

Uncle Dan, seeing his gardens lopped away,
Seeing his manured earth topple slowly in the stream,
Seeing his cows knee deep in yellow water,
His pigsties flooded, his flowerbeds drowned,
Seeing his prize leghorns swept down the stream,
Curses Father Missouri, impotently shakes
His fist at the forecloser, the treacherous skinflint;
Who takes what was loaned so very long ago,
And leaves puddles in his parlor, and useless lakes
In his fine pasture land.
Sees years of laboring turned into nothing.
Curses and shouts in his hoarse old voice
"Ain't got no right to act dat way at all!
No right at all!"
And the old river rolls on, sleepily to the gulf.

Checkers

Mojo Pete is bad,
Totes a gat,
Shoots to kill
At the drop of a hat.

    A man of God
    Is Deacon Cole,
    With the sins of the world
    Upon his soul.

But Saturdays
These strangers meet,
The man of God
And Mojo Pete.

    The barbershop loungers
    Lie no more
    Silently watching
    The weekly war.

And although Pete
Won't cuss at all
The deacon's words
Aren't biblical.

    "Pusson, what gits
    In de jam youse in,
    Better let somebody
    Play what kin."

"Be not puffed up
With anything,
My son. Trust God,
An' watch yo' King!"

    Mojo disdains
    His loud-voiced boss,
    Forgets his Missis,
    Rebbish, cross.

Deacon Cole forgets
A world drenched with sin,
Vexed by the trouble
His kingrow's in.

    The phonebell jangles
    Calling Pete;
    Pete won't budge
    Got de deacon beat.

And they play their game
Till the night grows old:
The Shepherd, and the lost lamb
From the fold.

Mose

Mose is black and evil
And damns his luck
Driving Mister Schwartz's
Big coal truck.

He's got no gal,
He's got no jack,
No fancy silk shirts
For his back.

But summer evenings,
Hard luck Mose
Goes in for all
The fun he knows.

On the corner kerb
With a sad quartette
His tenor peals
Like a clarinet.

O hit it Moses
Sing att thing
But Mose's mind
Goes wandering;—

And to the stars
Over the town
Floats, from a good man
Way, way down—

A soft song, filled
With a misery
Older than Mose
Will ever be.

After Winter

He snuggles his fingers
In the blacker loam
The lean months are done with,
The fat to come.

    His eyes are set
    On a brushwood-fire
    But his heart is soaring
    Higher and higher.

Though he stands ragged
An old scarecrow,
This is the way
His swift thoughts go,

    "Butter beans fo' Clara
    Sugar corn fo' Grace
    An' fo' de little feller
    Runnin' space.

"Radishes and lettuce
Eggplants and beets
Turnips fo' de winter
An' candied sweets.

    "Homespun tobacco
    Apples in de bin
    Fo' smokin' an' fo' cider
    When de folks draps in."

He thinks with the winter
His troubles are gone;
Ten acres unplanted
To raise dreams on.

    The lean months are done with,
    The fat to come.
    His hopes, winter wanderers,
    Hasten home.

"Butterbeans fo' Clara
Sugar corn fo' Grace
An' fo' de little feller
Runnin' space. . . ."

Pardners

Jim never had no luck wid de women,
No luck at all,—
Wife was a thin spry corkscrew woman
With a tongue lak a rusty awl;
One gal was a ton of meanness to him
An' ornery Jezebel,
Took his money and gave him back
A considabble heap of hell;
An' one was sweet an' frisky
Precisely lak a filly in clover,
Till off she ran with a railroad man
An' all uh dat was over.

On the coal truck Jim
Tells his pardner Tom
Jes' what de women done done to him;
He's a old old truck
An' he knows de road.

Says, "Watch 'em big boy
Les' dey does you hahm,
Draps you lak a coal truck
Draps its load;
Makes it hotter fo' you
Dan a pine knot fire;
Socks you lak David
Socked Goliah;
Watch 'em, bo,
Les' dey does you wrong,
Throws you fo' a row—
I means a row,—
Of de company's coalbins
Six miles long. . . ."

Slim Greer

Listen to the tale
Of Ole Slim Greer,
Waitines' devil
Waitin' here;

     Talkinges' guy
     An' biggest liar,
     With always a new lie
     On the fire.

Tells a tale
Of Arkansaw
That keeps the kitchen
In a roar;

     Tells in a long-drawled
     Careless tone,
     As solemn as a Baptist
     Parson's moan.

How he in Arkansaw
Passed for white,
An' he no lighter
Than a dark midnight.

     Found a nice white woman
     At a dance,
     Thought he was from Spain
     Or else from France;

Nobody suspicioned
Ole Slim Greer's race
But a Hill Billy, always
Roun' the place,

     Who called one day
     On the trustful dame
     An' found Slim comfy
     When he came.

The whites lef' the parlor
All to Slim
Which didn't cut
No ice with him,

> An' he started a-tinklin'
> Some mo'nful blues,
> An' a-pattin' the time
> With No. Fourteen shoes.

The cracker listened
An' then he spat
An' said, "No white man
Could play like that. . . ."

> The white jane ordered
> The tattler out;
> Then, female-like,
> Began to doubt,

Crept into the parlor
Soft as you please,
Where Slim was agitatin'
The ivories.

> Heard Slim's music—
> An' then, hot damn!
> Shouted sharp—"Nigger!"
> An' Slim said, "Ma'am?"

She screamed and the crackers
Swarmed up soon,
But found only echoes
Of his tune;

> 'Cause Slim had sold out
> With lightnin' speed;
> "Hope I may die, sir—
> Yes, indeed. . . ."

Slim Lands a Job?

Poppa Greer happened
  Down Arkansaw way,
An' ast for a job
  At Big Pete's Cafe.

        Big Pete was a six foot
          Hard-boiled man
        Wid a forty-four dungeon
          In his han'.

"Nigger, kin you wait?"
  Is what Pete ast;
Slim says, "Cap'n
  I'm jes' too fast."

        Pete says, "Dat's what
          I wants to hire;
        I got a slow nigger
          I'm gonna fire—

Don't 'low no slow nigger
  Stay roun' hyeah,
I plugs 'em wid my dungeon!"
  An' Slim says "Yeah?"

        A noise rung out
          In rush a man
        Wid a tray on his head
          An' one on each han'

Wid de silver in his mouf
  An' de soup plates in his vest
Pullin' a red wagon
  Wid all de rest. . . .

De man's said, "Dere's
  Dat slow coon now
Dat wuthless lazy waiter!"
  An' Slim says, "How?"

An' Slim threw his gears in
   Put it in high,
An' kissed his hand to Arkansaw,
   Sweetheart . . . good-bye!

Slim in Atlanta

Down in Atlanta,
  De whitefolks got laws
For to keep all de niggers
  From laughin' outdoors.

      Hope to Gawd I may die
        If I ain't speakin' truth
      Make de niggers do deir laughin'
        In a telefoam booth.

Slim Greer hit de town
  An' de rebs got him told,—
"Dontcha laugh on de street,
  If you want to die old."

      Den dey showed him de booth,
        An' a hundred shines
      In front of it, waitin'
        In double lines.

Slim thought his sides
  Would bust in two,
Yelled, "Lookout, everybody,
  I'm coming through!"

      Pulled de other man out,
        An' bust in de box,
      An' laughed four hours
        By de Georgia clocks.

Den he peeked through de door,
  An' what did he see?
Three hundred niggers there
  In misery.—

      Some holdin' deir sides,
        Some holdin' deir jaws,
      To keep from breakin'
        De Georgia laws.

An' Slim gave a holler,
  An' started again;
An' from three hundred throats
  Come a moan of pain.

    An' everytime Slim
      Saw what was outside,
    Got to whoopin' again
      Till he nearly died.

An' while de poor critters
  Was waitin' deir chance,
Slim laughed till dey sent
  Fo' de ambulance.

    De state paid de railroad
      To take him away;
    Den, things was as usural
      In Atlanta, Gee A.

Slim Hears "The Call"

I

Down at the barbershop
  Slim had the floor,
"Ain't never been so
  Far down before.

    "So ragged, I make a jaybird
      About to moult,
    Look like he got on gloves
      An' a overcoat.

"Got to walk backwards
  All de time
Jes' a-puttin' on front
  Wid a bare behime.

    "Been down to skin and bones
      Gittin' down to de gristle,
    So de call sounds louder
      Dan a factory whistle.

"Big holes is the onlies'
  Things in my pocket,
So bein' a bishop
  Is next on de docket.

    "Lawd, lawd, yas Lawd,
      I hears de call,
    An' I'll answer, good Lawd,
      Don't fret none atall.

"I heard it once
  An' I hears it again
Broadcast from the station
  W-I-N!

"Gonna be me a bishop
   That ain't no lie,
Get my cake down here,
   An' my pie in the sky.

II

     "Saw a buddy th' other day,
       Used to know him well
     Best coon-can player
       This side of hell.

"Had a voice as deep
   As a bellerin' bull,
Called hogs in a way
   Jes' beautiful.

     "Ran across him down
       In Caroline
     Folks interduced him
       As a 'great divine.'

"Had on a jimswinger
   Hangin' low,
An' a collar put on
   Hindparts befo'.

     "At first I jes' couldn't
       Fix his face,
     Then I remembered him dealin'
       In Shorty Joe's place.

" 'You got de advantage
   Of me, I fear—'
Then all of a sudden
   'My dear—Brother Greer!'

     "He let out a roar
       An' grabbed my hand:
     'Welcome, thou Pilgrim
       To our Pleasant Land!'

"Took me to a house
  Like de State Capitol:
'Jes' a shanty, not fit
  Fo' you, at all

    " 'Brother Greer, but if
      You'll stay wid me
    I'll try to make it up
      In hosspitality.'

"Called in his wife
  As purty as sin,
An' his secketary, twict
  As purty again.

    "When dey went out, he winked
      An' said—'Well, Slim?'
    An' he looked at me,
      An' I looked at him.

III

"Little fatter an' greasier
  Than when we had been
Side pardners together
  In de ways of sin.

    "Ran a great big school,
      Was de president,
    'Brother Greer, jus' see
      What de Lawd hath sent!'

"An' he de kind of guy
  Was sich a fool
Dey had to burn down de shack
  To get him out of school.

    "When de other pupils
      Was doin' history
    He was spellin' cat
      With a double p.

"Couldn't do no problems,
   But was pretty good
At beatin' out erasers
   An' bringin' in wood.

      "But he knew what side de bread
         You put de butter on,
         An' he could figger all right
         For number one.

"So here he was de head man
   Of de whole heap—
Wid dis solemn charge dat
   He had to keep:

      "A passel of Niggers
         From near an' far
         Bringin' in de sacred bucks
         Regular.

"Stayed wid him a while,
   Watched him do his stuff,
Wid a pint of good sense,
   An' a bushel of bluff.

      "Begged fo' his dyin' school
         At de conference
         Took up nine thousand dollars
         An' eighty cents.

"An' I swear, as sure
   As my name's Slim Greer,
He repohted to de school
   Sixteen dollars clear.

      " 'Expenses pretty high,'
         He said with a frown.
         An' de conference held
         In de very next town!

"Ordered the convention
　　To Los Angeles,
'Ain't no members out there,'
　　Said his enemies.

　　" 'Dat's jes' de reason
　　　　Why we gotta go,
　　　　Gotta missionize de heathen
　　　　　On de Western Sho'.

" 'Furrin parts is callin','
　　De Bishop says,
'Besides, I got a cravin'
　　Fo' oranges.'

　　"Filled a Pullman wid de delegates
　　　　He liked de best,
　　　　An' took a private plane
　　　　Fo' de Golden West.

"Las' words he said
　　As he rose in de air:
'Do lak me; take you' troubles
　　To de Lord in prayer.

　　" 'Brother Greer, do that,
　　　　An' you will see,
　　　　De Lawd'll be wid you,
　　　　　Like he's been wid me.'

IV

"I remembers his words
　　Now de North Wind blows
Like de Memphis special
　　Through my holy clothes.

　　"Now dat thinkin' of ham an' eggs
　　　　Makes me sick
　　　　Got me a longin'
　　　　Fo' de bishopric.

"I kin be a good bishop,
   I got de looks,
An' I ain't spoiled myself
   By readin' books.

      "Don't know so much
         'Bout de Holy Ghost,
      But I likes de long green
         Better'n most.

"I kin talk out dis worl'
   As you folks all know,
An' I'm good wid de women,
   Dey'll tell you so . . .

                    V

      "An' I says to all de Bishops,
         What is hearin' my song—
      Ef de cap fits you, brother,
         Put it on."

Slim in Hell

Slim Greer went to heaven;
  St. Peter said, "Slim,
You been a right good boy."
  An' he winked at him.

    "You been a travelin' rascal
      In yo' day.
    You kin roam once mo';
      Den you comes to stay.

"Put dese wings on yo' shoulders,
  An' save yo' feet."
Slim grin, and he speak up
  "Thankye, Pete."

    Den Peter say, "Go
      To Hell an' see,
    All dat is doing, and
      Report to me.

"Be sure to remember
  How everything go."
Slim say, "I be seein' yuh
  On de late watch, bo."

    Slim got to cavortin',
      Swell as you choose,
    Like Lindy in de "Spirit
      Of St. Louis Blues!"

He flew an' he flew,
  Till at last he hit
A hangar wid de sign readin'
  DIS IS IT.

Den he parked his wings,
   An' strolled aroun'
Gettin' used to his feet
   On de solid ground.

II

Big bloodhound came aroarin'
   Like Niagry Falls,
Sicked on by white devils
   In overhalls.

Now Slim warn't scared,
   Cross my heart, it's a fac',
An' de dog went on a bayin'
   Some po' devil's track.

Den Slim saw a mansion
   An' walked right in;
De Devil looked up
   Wid a sickly grin.

"Suttinly didn't look
   Fo' you, Mr. Greer,
How it happen you comes
   To visit here?"

Slim say—"Oh, jes' thought
   I'd drap by a spell."
"Feel at home, seh, an' here's
   De keys to Hell."

Den he took Slim around
   An' showed him people
Raisin' hell as high as
   De First Church Steeple.

Lots of folks fightin'
   At de roulette wheel,
Like old Rampart Street,
   Or leastwise Beale.

Showed him bawdy houses
　An' cabarets,
Slim thought of New Orleans
　An' Memphis days.

　　Each devil was busy
　　　Wid a devilish broad,
　　An' Slim cried, "Lawdy,
　　　Lawd, Lawd, Lawd."

Took him in a room
　Where Slim see
De preacher wid a brownskin
　On each knee.

　　Showed him giant stills,
　　　Going everywhere
　　Wid a passel of devils,
　　　Stretched dead drunk there.

Den he took him to de furnace
　Dat some devils was firing,
Hot as hell, an' Slim start
　A mean presspirin';

　　White devils wid pitchforks
　　　Threw black devils on,
　　Slim thought he'd better
　　　Be gittin' along.

An' he say—"Dis makes
　Me think of home—
Vicksburg, Little Rock, Jackson,
　Waco, and Rome."

　　Den de devil gave Slim
　　　De big Ha-Ha;
　　An' turned into a cracker,
　　　Wid a sheriff's star.

Slim ran fo' his wings,
  Lit out from de groun'
Hauled it back to St. Peter,
  Safety boun'.

III

St. Peter said, "Well,
  You got back quick.
How's de devil? An' what's
  His latest trick?"

An' Slim say, "Peter,
  I really cain't tell,
De place was Dixie
  Dat I took for Hell."

Then Peter say, "You must
  Be crazy, I vow,
Where'n hell dja think Hell *was*,
  Anyhow?

"Git on back to de yearth,
  Cause I got de fear,
You'se a leetle too dumb,
  Fo' to stay up here . . ."

New Steps

New steps
O my Lawd
New steps a-climbin'
New steps a-climbin' to de little Church do'—

Sister Annie
Sees Brother Luck a-grinnin' once mo',
Sees Victory wid shinin' wings
Flappin' obbertop de low down Foot.
New steps a-climbin' on Annie's Church
Risin', a-risin',
From de mud o' sin;
Brother Luck grinnin' a moughty grin;
Sister Annie
Trusts at de las' her boy, her boy
Gonna be saved from ruin.
Shakes her gray head, straightens up tall,
Struts herself down to the sinful Foot,
Place of de scandalizin', evil doin',
No furder off than a good stone's throw.
She's back on speakin' terms wid fly Miss Joy;
Happy at las'—
New steps a-climbin' to de little Church do'—

Lawd—
Good times, seems like, ain't fuh las'—
Nebber de real good times, dey ain't—
What does she see at de sinful Foot
But ole Ben Ames
May de devil scorch his ornery hide
Puttin' green paint
On his poolroom den,
An' big white letters on his window glass—
An' the dingy house on the other side
Of de muddy road, of de sinful road,
Runnin' over wid jazz an' scarlet noise
(Snatchin' from de church pews all de men
Aw—let 'em go—but de growin' boys!)
Sportin' new lace next the dirty panes,

Downstairs, upstairs,
New lace curtains.

Up de new steps that meetin' night
Sister Annie drug a heavy an' a weary load.
New steps a-climbin'—
O my Lawd
Lace curtains snow white
Snow white curtains
O my Lawd
Upstairs, downstairs,

New steps
O my Lawd. . . .

Convict

Jim is on the gang,
Working on the road;
Goes out in the morning
With the prison load;

Sees the little shacks
Mist covered, dim. . . .
And another daybreak
Comes back to him,

That brought him to handcuffs,
And a dingy cell,
Daytime on the highways,
Nights in hell.

When the truck rolls back
As the sun goes down,
Jim sees what he is used to
In Shantytown.

Sleeping hounds everywhere,
Flies crawling thick,
Grown ups drunken
And children sick.

Three long months
Till he takes his ease,
With their filth and squalor
And miseries. . . .

Jim as the night falls
Gets his view
Of the longed for heaven
He's returning to. . . .

Strange Legacies

One thing you left with us, Jack Johnson.
One thing before they got you.

You used to stand there like a man,
Taking punishment
With a golden, spacious grin;
Confident.
Inviting big Jim Jeffries, who was boring in:
"Heah ah is, big boy; yuh sees whah Ise at.
Come on in. . . ."

Thanks, Jack, for that.

John Henry, with your hammer;
John Henry, with your steel driver's pride,
You taught us that a man could go down like a man,
Sticking to your hammer till you died.
Sticking to your hammer till you died.

Brother,
When, beneath the burning sun
The sweat poured down and the breath came thick,
And the loaded hammer swung like a ton
And the heart grew sick;
You had what we need now, John Henry.
Help us get it.

So if we go down
Have to go down
We go like you, brother,
'Nachal' men. . . .

Old nameless couple in Red River Bottom,
Who have seen floods gutting out your best loam,
And the boll weevil chase you
Out of your hard-earned home,
Have seen the drought parch your green fields,
And the cholera stretch your porkers out dead;
Have seen year after year
The commissary always a little in the lead;

Even you said
That which we need
Now in our time of fear,—
Routed your own deep misery and dread,
Muttering, beneath an unfriendly sky,
"Guess we'll give it one mo' try.
Guess we'll give it one mo' try."

Revelations

"Why do folks call you Revelations?"
"It used to be because I preached from that Book. But now because I reveals."
TALKS WITH THE VILLAGE HALFWIT

I shall recall
As a sinister omen,
That which was pity
For full-bosomed women,—

That which was laughter
For idling men;
Bundle of rags,
And tattered brain,

Cadaverous cheeks,
And bloodshot eyes,
And wide mouth mumbling
Obscenities,

Or echoes from childhood's
Store of rhyme,
Or scraps of religion
Near sublime. . . .

I shall remember
Troubledly, long,
His cracked voice
Wheezing out his song:

"You gotta walk that lonesome valley,
You gotta walk it by yo'self,
Nobody heah can a-walk it for you
You gotta walk it by yo'self."

And this comment
From wisdom not his own
"Man wanta live,
Man wanta find himself

Man gotta learn
How to go alone."

Always now with me
The halfwit's text,
Sour truth for my wits
Poor, perplexed,

"If man's life goes
Beyond the bone
Man must go lonely
And alone,
Unhelped, unhindered
On his own. . . ."

Riverbank Blues

A man git his feet set in a sticky mudbank,
A man git dis yellow water in his blood,
No need for hopin', no need for doin',
Muddy streams keep him fixed for good.

Little Muddy, Big Muddy, Moreau and Osage,
Little Mary's, Big Mary's, Cedar Creek,
Flood deir muddy water roundabout a man's roots,
Keep him soaked and stranded and git him weak.

Lazy sun shinin' on a little cabin,
Lazy moon glistenin' over river trees;
Ole river whisperin', lappin' 'gainst de long roots:
"Plenty of rest and peace in these. . . ."

Big mules, black loam, apple and peach trees,
But seems lak de river washes us down
Past de rich farms, away from de fat lands,
Dumps us in some ornery riverbank town.

Went down to the river, sot me down an' listened,
Heard de water talkin' quiet, quiet lak an' slow:
"Ain' no need fo' hurry, take yo' time, take yo' time. . . ."
Heard it sayin'—*"Baby, hyeahs de way life go. . . ."*

Dat is what it tole me as I watched it slowly rollin',
But somp'n way inside me rared up an' say,
"Better be movin' . . . better be travelin' . . .
Riverbank'll git you ef you stay. . . ."

Towns are sinkin' deeper, deeper in de riverbank,
Takin' on de ways of deir sulky Ole Man—
Takin' on his creepy ways, takin' on his evil ways,
"Bes' git way, a long way . . . whiles you can.

"Man got his sea too lak de Mississippi
Ain't got so long for a whole lot longer way,
Man better move some, better not git rooted
Muddy water fool you, ef you stay. . . ."

Part Three

TIN ROOF BLUES

I'm got de tin roof blues,
Got dese sidewalks on my mind.
TIN ROOF BLUES

for Poodle Williams

Tin Roof Blues

I'm goin' where de Southern crosses top de C. & O.
I'm goin' where de Southern crosses top de C. & O.
I'm goin' down de country cause I cain't stay here no mo'.

Goin' where de Norfolk Western curves jes' lak de river bends,
Where de Norfolk Western swing around de river bends,
Goin' where de people stacks up mo' lak friends.

Leave 'is dirty city, take my foot up in my hand,
Dis do-dirty city, take my foot up in my hand,
Git down to de livin' what a man kin understand.

Gang of dicties here, an' de rest wants to git dat way,
Dudes an' dicties, others strive to git dat way,
Put pennies on de numbers from now unto de jedgement day.

I'm got de tin roof blues, got dese sidewalks on my mind,
De tin roof blues, dese lonesome sidewalks on my mind,
I'm goin' where de shingles covers people mo' my kind.

Effie

She who was easy for any chance lover,
Whose frequent laugh rang flaccid and shrill;
She, finding death at last, the dazed fret over,
Lies here so oddly stern for once, and still.

Put her away, and put away with her
What she has now of harshness and strength,
She who was clay for any clumsy sculptor
Becomes inflexible; fixed of form at length.

She who would veer with any passing wind
Like a rusty vane with rickety ways,
She is aloof now, and seems—oh, so determined;
And that is the Paradise crowning her days.

Children's Children

When they hear
These songs, born of the travail of their sires,
Diamonds of song, deep buried beneath the weight
Of dark and heavy years;
They laugh.

When they hear
Saccharine melodies of loving and its fevers,
Soft-flowing lies of love everlasting;
Conjuring divinity out of gross flesh itch;
They sigh
And look goggle-eyed
At one another.

They have forgotten, they have never known,
Long days beneath the torrid Dixie sun
In miasma'd riceswamps;
The chopping of dried grass, on the third go round
In strangling cotton;
Wintry nights in mud-daubed makeshift huts,
With these songs, sole comfort.

They have forgotten
What had to be endured—

That they, babbling young ones,
With their paled faces, coppered lips,
And sleek hair cajoled to Caucasian straightness,
Might drown the quiet voice of beauty
With sensuous stridency;

And might, on hearing these memoirs of their sires,
Giggle,
And nudge each other's satin clad
Sleek sides. . . .

Mecca

Maggie came up from Spartansburg,
   Tom from Martinique,
They met at a Harlem house-rent stomp,
   And were steadies in a week.

Tom bought him a derby and pearl gray spats,
   When his first week's work was done,
Mag bought herself a sealskin coat,
   Hot in more ways than one.

O milk and honey of the promised land!
   When Sunday rolls round again,
Lady Margaret, lord! . . . She tips for fair,
   And Lord Thomas . . . twirls his cane.

Chillen Get Shoes

Hush little Lily,
  Don't you cry;
You'll get your silver slippers
  Bye and bye.

Moll wears silver slippers
  With red heels,
And men come to see her
  In automobiles.

Lily walks wretched,
  Dragging her doll,
Worshipping stealthily
  Good-time Moll;

Envying bitterly
  Moll's fine clothes,
And her plump legs clad
  In openwork hose.

Don't worry, Lily,
  Don't you cry;
You'll be like Moll, too,
  Bye and bye.

Funeral

The garnish of the world's acclaim
Was thrown upon him when he died.

To pay eye service to his fame,
Crowds gathered on the clay hillside.

But she who bore his honored name
Stood by aloof, defiant-eyed.

And on and on in his singsong way
The preacher droned, as preachers must,

Of the tenant who leased this heavy clay—
Ashes to ashes, dust to dust. . . .

The woman laughed as they led her away:
"He will be true to this bed, I trust."

Harlem Street Walkers

Why do they walk so tragical
Oh, never mind, when they are in
The grateful grave, each whitened skull
Will grin. . . .

Sporting Beasley

Good glory, give a look at Sporting Beasley
Strutting, oh my Lord.

    Tophat cocked one side his bulldog head,
    Striped four-in-hand, and in his buttonhole
    A red carnation; Prince Albert coat
    Form-fitting, corset like; vest snugly filled,
    Gray morning trousers, spotless and full-flowing,
    White spats and a cane.

Step it, Mr. Beasley, oh step it till the sun goes down.

    Forget the snippy clerks you wait upon,
    Tread clouds of glory above the heads of pointing children,
    Oh, Mr. Peacock, before the drab barnfowl of the world.

    Forget the laughter when at the concert
    You paced down the aisle, your majesty,
    Down to Row A, where you pulled out your opera glasses.

    Majesty. . . .

    It's your turn now, Sporting Beasley,
    Step it off.

    The world is a ragbag; the world
    Is full of heathens who haven't seen the light;
    Do it, Mr. Missionary.

Great glory, give a look.

    Oh Jesus, when this brother's bill falls due,
    When he steps off the chariot
    And flicks the dust from his patent leathers with his silk handkerchief,
    When he stands in front of the jasper gates, patting his tie,

    And then paces in
    Cane and knees working like well-oiled slow-timed pistons;

Lord help us, give a *look* at him.

Don't make him dress up in no night gown, Lord.
Don't put no fuss and feathers on his shoulders, Lord.

Let him know it's heaven.

Let him keep his hat, his vest, his elkstooth, and everything.

Let him have his spats and cane
Let him have his spats and cane.

Cabaret

(1927, Black & Tan Chicago)

Rich, flashy, puffy-faced,
Hebrew and Anglo-Saxon,
The overlords sprawl here with their glittering darlings.
The smoke curls thick, in the dimmed light
Surreptitiously, deaf-mute waiters
Flatter the grandees,
Going easily over the rich carpets,
Wary lest they kick over the bottles
Under the tables.

The jazzband unleashes its frenzy.

> *Now, now,*
> *To it, Roger; that's a nice doggie,*
> *Show your tricks to the gentlemen.*

The trombone belches, and the saxophone
Wails curdlingly, the cymbals clash,
The drummer twitches in an epileptic fit

> Muddy water
> Round my feet
> Muddy water

The chorus sways in.
The 'Creole Beauties from New Orleans'
(By way of Atlanta, Louisville, Washington, Yonkers,
With stop-overs they've used nearly all their lives)
Their creamy skin flushing rose warm,
O, le bal des belles quarterounes!
Their shapely bodies naked save
For tattered pink silk bodices, short velvet tights,
And shining silver-buckled boots;
Red bandannas on their sleek and close-clipped hair;
To bring to mind (aided by the bottles under the tables)
Life upon the river—

Muddy water, river sweet

(Lafitte the pirate, instead,
And his doughty diggers of gold)

There's peace and happiness there
I declare

(In Arkansas,
Poor half-naked fools, tagged with identification numbers,
Worn out upon the levees,
Are carted back to the serfdom
They had never left before
And may never leave again)

Bee—dap—ee—DOOP, dee—ba—dee—BOOP

The girls wiggle and twist

Oh you too,
Proud high-stepping beauties,
Show your paces to the gentlemen.
A prime filly, seh.
What am I offered, gentlemen, gentlemen. . . .

I've been away a year today
To wander and roam
I don't care if it's muddy there

(Now that the floods recede,
What is there left the miserable folk?
Oh time in abundance to count their losses,
There is so little else to count.)

Still it's my home, sweet home

From the lovely throats
Moans and deep cries for home:
Nashville, Toledo, Spout Springs, Boston,
Creoles from Germantown;—
The bodies twist and rock;
The glasses are filled up again. . . .

(In Mississippi
The black folk huddle, mute, uncomprehending,
Wondering 'how come the good Lord
Could treat them this a way')

        shelter
    Down in the Delta

(Along the Yazoo
The buzzards fly over, over, low,
Glutted, but with their scrawny necks stretching,
Peering still.)

    I've got my toes turned Dixie ways
    Round that Delta let me laze

The band goes mad, the drummer throws his sticks
At the moon, a *papier-mâché* moon,
The chorus leaps into weird posturings,
The firm-fleshed arms plucking at grapes to stain
Their coralled mouths; seductive bodies weaving
Bending, writhing, turning

    My heart cries out for
    MUDDY WATER

(Down in the valleys
The stench of the drying mud
Is a bitter reminder of death.)

    Dee da dee D A A A A H

Part Four

VESTIGES

When I was one-and-twenty
I heard a wise man say—
A. E. HOUSMAN

for Rose Anne

Salutamus

O Gentlemen the time of Life is short.
HENRY IV, PART I

The bitterness of days like these we know;
Much, much we know, yet cannot understand
What was our crime that such a searing brand
Not of our choosing, keeps us hated so.
Despair and disappointment only grow,
Whatever seeds are planted from our hand,
What though some roads wind through a gladsome land?
It is a gloomy path that we must go.

And yet we know relief will come some day
For these seared breasts; and lads as brave again
Will plant and find a fairer crop than ours.
It must be due our hearts, our minds, our powers;
These are the beacons to blaze out the way.
We must plunge onward; onward, gentlemen. . . .

To a Certain Lady, in Her Garden

(For Anne Spencer)

Lady, my lady, come from out the garden,
Clay-fingered, dirty-smocked, and in my time
I too shall learn the quietness of Arden,
Knowledge so long a stranger to my rhyme.

What were more fitting than your springtime task?
Here, close-engirdled by your vines and flowers
Surely there is no other grace to ask,
No better cloister from the bickering hours.

A step beyond, the dingy streets begin
With all their farce, and silly tragedy—
But here, unmindful of the futile din
You grow your flowers, far wiser certainly.

You and your garden sum the same to me,
A sense of strange and momentary pleasure,
And beauty snatched—oh, fragmentarily
Perhaps, yet who can boast of other seizure?

Oh, you have somehow robbed, I know not how,
The secret of the loveliness of these
Whom you have served so long. Oh, shameless, now
You flaunt the winnings of your thieveries.

Thus, I exclaim against you, profiteer. . . .
For purpled evenings spent in pleasing toil,
Should you have gained so easily the dear
Capricious largesse of the miser soil?

Colorful living in a world grown dull,
Quiet sufficiency in weakling days,
Delicate happiness, more beautiful
For lighting up belittered, grimy ways—

Surely I think I shall remember this,
You in your old, rough dress, bedaubed with clay,

Your smudgy face parading happiness,
Life's puzzle solved. Perhaps, in turn, you may

One time, while clipping bushes, tending vines,
(Making your brave, sly mock at dastard days),
Laugh gently at these trivial, truthful lines—
And that will be sufficient for my praise.

Challenge

I said, in drunken pride of youth and you,
That mischief-making Time would never dare
Play his ill-humored tricks upon us two,
Strange and defiant lovers that we were.
I said that even Death, Highwayman Death,
Could never master lovers such as we,
That even when his clutch had throttled breath,
My hymns would float in praise, undauntedly.

I did not think such words were bravado.
Oh, I think honestly we knew no fear,
Of Time or Death. We loved each other so.
And thus, with you believing me, I made
My prophecies, rebellious, unafraid. . . .
And that was foolish, wasn't it, my dear?

Telling Fortunes

Oh you were quite the gypsy on that night. . . .
The backyard peachtree tapped insistently
Against the window, and the flickering light
Set eerie shades dancing fantastically.
You with a red cloth on your heavy hair
Tinting your face with darkrose mysteries
Shuffled and cut the cards with an old crone's care
Delightful as ever with your mimicries.

"This card a trip," you said. "You go your way,
Another foolish way, boy, joked by men,
Whether alone or not it does not say."
And this, "Beware of women with dark eyes,"
You teased; I laughed. . . . Oh you were very wise
Who could have understood such wisdom then?

Rain

Outside the cold, cold night; the dripping rain. . . .
The water gurgles loosely in the eaves,
The savage lashes stripe the rattling pane
And beat a tattoo on November leaves.
The lamp wick gutters, and the last log steams
Upon the ash-filled hearth. Chill grows the room.
The ancient clock ticks creakily and seems
A fitting portent of the gathering gloom.

This is a night we planned. This place is where
One day, we would be happy; where the light
Should tint your shoulders and your wild flung hair.—
Whence we would—oh, we planned a merry morrow—
Recklessly part ways with the old hag, Sorrow. . . .

Outside the dripping rain; the cold, cold night.

Return

I have gone back in boyish wonderment
To things that I had foolishly put by. . . .
Have found an alien and unknown content
In seeing how some bits of cloud-filled sky
Are framed in bracken pools; through chuckling hours
Have watched the antic frogs, or curiously
Have numbered all the unnamed, vagrant flowers,
That fleck the unkempt meadows, lavishly.

Or where a headlong toppling stream has stayed
Its racing, lulled to quiet by the song
Bursting from out the thick-leaved oaken shade,
There I have lain while hours sauntered past—
I have found peacefulness somewhere at last,
Have found a quiet needed for so long.

Nous n'irons plus au bois . . .

Oh, I shall meet your friends, and chatter on
As trivially, as sillily as they,
My talk resembling much the rattling way
Of an incessant mower on a lawn.
Oh I shall smirk and prink and scrape and fawn
And listen to the nothings that they say
And answer less. And for a juvenile play
Shall all matured integrity be gone.

And there are very many things beside
That I shall do. And one of these will be
When you reward me for rank cowardice.
I shall call back, to fretting memory,
A hut, pine-circled, on a wild hillside,
And peace thrown lavishly away—*for this*. . . .

Thoughts of Death

Thoughts of death
Crowd over my happiness
Like dark clouds
Over the silver sickle of the moon.

> *Death comes to some*
> *Like a grizzled gangster*
> *Clubbing in the night;*
> *To some*
> *Like an obstinate captain*
> *Steadily besieging barriers;*
> *To some like a brown adder*
> *Lurking in violet-speckled underbrush;*
> *To some*
> *Like a gentle nurse*
> *Taking their toys and stroking their hot brows.*
>
> *Death will come to you, I think,*
> *Like an old shrewd gardener*
> *Culling his rarest blossom. . . .*

Against That Day

When your brave eyes are stopped with dust,
And on your glittering auburn hair
Is laid a coating of thick rust,
When there is clutching silence where
Was once the flair of mirth, and gone
Is all your arrant nimble grace,
And worms preposterous feed upon
The sweet flesh of your lovely face;
When you at last accommodate
Your sinuous body to a bed
Narrow and damp and starkly straight,
With rubble pillowing up your head;
What will there be then to rebel
Against Time's crazy tyranny,
What wretched substitute to tell
Your loveliness and bravery?
What but these verses will there be
To rail at Old Time for the wrong
He did to you, he does to me? . . .
And these will last not overlong. . . .

Mill Mountain

The moon is but a lantern set by some
Old truant shepherd to light up a field
Where strange and brilliant stones sparkle at one
From the blue darkness. . . . A scattering of sheep
Tread over these bright gems, in scampering
Across the level stretches to the place
Where glows the lantern with a dazzling light.
They rush on past, fleecy and gray and noiseless.
Strange pastoral for poor city dwellers, child.

And see, below. . . . So many more bright stars,
It seems, and golden where these gems are jade
Glint merrily. . . . Could you believe that is
Our city—*that*—the distant fairyland?
So many stars—so golden—and so far.
Such little time for such a startling change.
A brief while climbing hills, and what we knew
Too well as turbulence has grown at last
To beauty—quiet, almost faerylike.
Somewhere down there, I know that you are doubtful
And I am too, *"in such a night as this*
When the sweet wind did gently kiss the trees"
Somewhere I must insist, we lived all day to day,
And all day for so many yesterdays,
And probably will live so many morrows.
Will it not help when those drab morrows come
With their same burdens you have known so long,
And which, poor tired child, you look on as
Inevitable, unlikely to be shared
Even by me—will it not help to know
That they in such a very little time
Can be relinquished, and almost forgotten?
See how the city streets are lined with light,
And see the figures intricately stenciled
With pricks of gold. . . . Child, is it not a loom
On which some friendly fairy weaves for us
Beauty by night, for daily ugliness?
Those slowly creeping lights, some realists
Would tell us are the headlights of real cars
But we know better. . . . Are you listening?

What has become at last, my frightened child,
Of that brown city that we knew by day?
What of its squalor, of its pettiness—
What of its blatant noises and its dirt—
Its crying children and its fretting grind—
And hectic love close pent in sultry rooms?
What matter those things here, where there is peace,
And cleanliness, where a bright moon looks down
Untroubledly from a rich blue sky, where winds
That set the lofty cedar tops to creaking
And whisper in the underbrush, are all
The sounds that break our quietude, my musing.

Such, such a little time, and we can put away
Intolerable things, and we can find at last
Place for communion, place for holy things
Bringing oblivion to trivial cares.
See, Cinderella, all the staring searchlights
That flank the railroads too officiously
Grope in the dark for us. But all their zeal
Will one day mean so little. We'll return
When we well please then. Almost midnight, child.
I nearly had forgotten the tomorrow. . . .
Oh, but tomorrow. . . . We have learned tonight
That there are havens from all desperate seas,
And every ruthless war rounds into peace.
It seems to me that Love can be that peace
However stormy or warlike Life has seemed.
What do you think? Why do you never answer?
Asleep so soon . . . And what a quiet breathing.

Sleep, child. . . . It's better than these words of mine.
Words that I meant sincerely to be rich
Of healing for your fever—that have turned
To empty words, apparently so poor.
Sleep on. What else is there for you,—but sleep?

THE LAST RIDE OF WILD BILL

to the Dunbar Independents
(who prodded my tall tales)

Axe
Bill
Forty-five
Flap
Ike
Lancess
Sam
In memory of Charlie and Ralph

The Last Ride of Wild Bill

I. THE CHALLENGE

The new Chief of police
Banged his desk
Called in the force, and swore
That the number-running game was done
And Wild Bill
Would ride no more.

The rumor
Spread quickly
Caught up with Wild Bill,
In Darktown
At his rendezvous.
It left him untouched
Left him cool,
He went on shooting
His game of pool.
He ran up fifteen
And then he spat.
"Rack 'em up," he said.
His voice was flat.
He put a lead slug
In the telephone
He spoke to the Chief
In a tone
Colorless, sad,
As if what he had
To say was hurting him
Pretty bad.
"I just heard the news
You spread over town.
I raise you one,
I call your bluff.
Your cops
Are not quite tough
Enough.
And you ain't so smart,
I will be bound,

To run the
Great Wild Bill
To ground.
I'd like you to know,
What I thought you knew,
You have bit off more
Than you'll ever chew.
As long as loose change
Is in this town
Wild Bill
Will still
Run the numbers down."

II. THE NEWS

The news flashed.
Messenger boys dashed,
Hither and yon,
Yon and hither.
The town was in one hell of a dither.
Big business got the jitters
Did the hootchie-kootchie
From Stone Mountain down
To the Chattahoochee
From Marietta,
To Decatur,
From the muckamucks
And the highty-tighty,
Down to the people on relief.
The talk was about
The Gawd-almighty
Brass-bound impudence
Of the Chief.

The slot machine boys
Deserted their slots;
The pool-room boys
Scratched their shots;
The beer-garden boys
Turned down their pots.
Even Madame Mamie

When she heard
Suspended business
Till further word.
Tailoring places
And beauty salons
Wondered how
They could carry on.
Till the Chamber of Commerce
Released a release:
"Wild Bill's stock
Is due to rise;
Carloading will increase
Likewise."

"Lay your money where your heart is,"
Said big business.

Confidence mounted
To the skies.

III. CIVIC RESPONSE

The folks responded with civic pride:
In North Side Drive,
On Ponce de Leon,
All over the city's
Ritzy side
Many a Dixie matron
And her scion
Wagered that Wild Bill
Still
Would ride.
In Pittsburgh section,
Beaver Slide,
Ward Eight, West End and
Summer Hill,
Side bets were made
And big dough laid
And the odds were heavy
On Wild Bill.
These were the people

That the bug had bit,
Betting now
On a sure-fire hit:
Kiwanians and Rotarians
Daughters, Sons, Cousins
Of Confederate Veterans,
The Kleagle of the Ku Klux Klan,
The Knights of the Pantry
And Dames of the Pan,
The aristocrats, the landed gentry,
The cracker, and the jigaboo
Hoi-polloi
All seemed to think well
Of their boy,
Were eager to lay
Their bucks on Bill.

On Druid Hill
An old-stock cavalier tried to bet
His yard-boy part of his back-pay due
But Mose he believed in Wild Bill too.
A U.D.C.
Gave five to three
To her three-in-one-mammy-laundress-cook,
Down at Five Points
They set up a scoreboard,
To tell folks the newest odds
On the book.
Money was talking
Five dollars to two
Said Wild Bill would bring
The numbers through.

IV. THE DAY: THE CHIEF

Into his office
The new Chief came
Not chipper, but game,
Not running away.
On his desk
A telegram lay:

"Ride my route
Again today;
Start at noon,
End at three.
Guess it will have
To be you and me."
The telegram was C.O.D.
The Chief's bald head
Flushed beet red.
His jaw clicked shut
On the masticated stogie butt.

The office was sinister
And still.
The new electric time piece ticked
Off the last few hours till
The Chief's appointment with Wild Bill.

The Chief was stumped
But he wasn't licked.
He watched the clock
Then something clicked.
"I got it," he said.
He fingered through the telephone book.
His breath came fast.
His fingers shook.
He talked to himself.
Nervous, grim,
"Since it will have to be
Me or him,
I choose him.
And him it will be
By hook or crook."
He took the telephone
Off the hook.

V. THE DAY: WILD BILL

At eleven-thirty
Wild Bill was ready,
His voice was steady

But his temper dirty.
He got up from his business lunch.
They fixed him up
A Planter's Punch.

He looked at the cherry and the lime with scorn,
Threw the fruit mixture in the sink
"No salad for me,
When I drink I drink."
Got a two-by-four scantling for a bracer,
Drank a tumbler of corn
With rye for a chaser.
He looked at the clock,
Ten minutes to go.
He looked at his jumper
Who was looking low.
He said: "Today's run
May be tough.
Guess I'll make
My own jumps today."
The jumper spoke up
Quick and gruff:
"The hell you say
And the hell you will,
Reckon I'm sticking from now until."
Bill looked at the kid
And said "O.K."
At eleven forty-eight,
They walked out to the parked V 8
He waved to the gang
Gathered at the door
"Be back on the dot
At half past four."

He kicked his tires
And they were solid,
Looked at his gas gauge
Gas O.K.
He stepped on his starter,
It turned over easy.
Wild Bill and his rider
Were on their way.

The schools might as well
Have declared holiday;
In gala array
With ribbons and banners,
Munching on peanuts
And bananas
The kids were out
Lining the route
That Wild Bill
Was known to ride;
Even the principals weren't inside.

From Oglethorpe, Emory, and Georgia Tech,
Spelman, Morehouse, and Morris Brown,
The collegians were on hand;
Each institute of learning
Had its band.
The one from Agnes Scott
Was particularly hot.
Cheerleaders pranced
And crowds snake-danced.
It was quite intellectual
And advanced.
Even the theologues
Came from Gammon
To see the Law
Give war
To Mammon.
The flocks
Of the Ebelezer A.M.E.
And the Holy Jumpers were side by side,
Forgetting their battles
To see Bill Ride.
The Canon and the Dean
Of the Diocese of Infinitesimal Believers
Were out in their swallowtails and beavers,
Bestowing their blessing
On the scene.

Banks were shut,
Stores
Closed doors,
The wheels of industry
Were still:
The city fathers' tribute
To Wild Bill.

VII. THE CHASE: FIRST PART

The hounds crossed a false trail
In West End,
They bayed long,
Loud and wrong:
The fox was elsewhere
Idling along.
But on Pearson Road
They struck the trace,
Right after Bill
Had left the place.
The scent was new,
Foolproof and true,
So they settled doggedly
To the chase.

The fox, he grinned
He thought his tricks
Could save him from
A tighter fix.

But the hunter who ran
At the head of the pack
Was a master trailer
From way back.
And once the real run
Was begun,
The fox knew it wasn't
Just for fun.
So he soared up the hill,
Roared down the vale,

With the hounds a-baying
On his trail,
A bit too close
Upon his tail.

The sound of the sirens
Long and loud
Reached all the way
To the gathered crowd
Anxious, ready.
From the steady
Resolute, collected baying
They knew the Chief's pack
Wasn't playing.

But still they knew
Their Wild Bill too.

VIII. THE CHASE: SECOND PART

Up on Ashby
The cops were gaining
Wild Bill sure
Seemed out of luck,
When out from an alley
Sam Johnson backed
In the remnants of a
Punch-drunk truck.
It settled in the middle of the tracks,
Right in front of the police car.
"Sorry, cap'n, but I do declah,
Havin' a little trouble here
Wid my truck.
I believe to my soul
De clutch done stuck."
The Chief he fumed and the cop he swore,
Like Sam had never heard before,
But the stuck—
Clutch truck
Was there to stay.

And the fox
Was eight good blocks
Away.

When Bill turned off
Of West Fair
They thought they had got him bottled there
Slicker than slick.
The usual thoroughfare
Was blind.
A truck of bricks broadside before
Two runabouts behind.
But Bill wasn't born to die in a bottle,
Quicker than quick
He opened the throttle;
Spun into a yard at fifty-three,
Backed out at sixty-four
Threw her in first at seventy-five
And side-swiped the law.
He turned the nearest corner
With three wheels in the air
Then settled back into his speed
And got the hell
Away from there.

At Grady Square
Wild Bill's need was sore again,
So a veteran
Who had stayed in front
Of Sherman, marching to the sea,
Tottered out,
And sang about
The Dixie where he wished to be.
He soon collected a singing throng.

The police came up at the second verse,
Halted, saluted, uncovered, and stood
Like the others of that multitude,
Lifting their voices in the song,
Solemn, sad,
Their harmonizing wasn't bad.
And when
The hymn had got to the long amen,

Wild Bill's chances
Were all to the good.
He was four miles from
That neighborhood.
"Look away, look away,
Look away, Dixie Land!"

Another Negro
Down at Decatur,
Held up the chase
A little later.
Waved his arms
Like a semaphore
Went into a dance,
Flagged down the Law.

They pulled up murderous,
But they pulled up quick.
The fellow talked slow,
Meek and low:
"You see it's like dis,
My wife is sick
And when I heard de siren blow
I thought dat dis was de ambulance.
I wants to beg yo' pardon
In advance."
They cursed him fierce,
They wished him dead.
They bent a night-stick
On his head.
He needed the ambulance
Really then.
But Wild Bill had been saved
Again.

IX. THE CHASE: THIRD PART

The fox heard the dogs bay
Far away
They had lost the scent
And they were spent

Danger was past
And at long last
The fox could safely head
For his den.
Wild Bill had foiled
The Law again.

He eased up his foot
Let the engine dally
It purred along
Like Rudy Vallee;
He turned to his jumper
By his side.
The jumper was beaming
And his grin was wide.
They checked
The collect
And were satisfied.
They had picked up the bags
As per schedule:
Third Baptist Church,
The Vocational School,
The Registrar's office
At the City Jail,
Braxton Bragg's statue
On the horse's tail,
Behind a hedge on the Courthouse lawn,
The Parish-House of the Cathedral
Of Saint John
Who saw the holy number
And so on.

From Sub-Station Q
On Auburn Avenue
From Sub-Station L
On the Stone Mountain Road
From the office of the Emergency Relief—
"Ain't missed nary one,"
The jumper told his chief.
From the H L A, the C C C,
The I B W O Z E,
The branch of the N-Double O.C.P.

The A.S.F. and the D. C. V.
The K. K. K.
All were registered
O. K.

Then Bill saw a bag
In a new place.
He looked at his jumper
With doubt in his face.
"Must be a new agent
We ain't checked.
But the bag is fat
And it looks correct,
It's a territory
We don't know,
But we better make a clean sweep
As we go."
The jumper brought it to him
Laid it on his knee,
It was heavier than a bag
Had right to be.
Bill held it to his ear,
Heard something tick,
Then he understood
The Chief's last trick.
As he threw it from him,
He heard the roar;
And then the great Bill
Knew no more.

X. THE LAST COLLECT

When he came to,
His bus was hitting,
Lickety-splitting,
Hell bent on wheels
Down a straight dark road;
Only one battered headlight glowed.
His jumper was missing
And so was his car.

He looked to the right,
It was black as tar.
Looked to the left,
Blacker there.
The wheel was clammy,
The air was damp.
"Don't know where I'm going
But I've sure come far,
This must be the swamp
Near Florida."
Suddenly,
A red light glowed,
Like the world on fire
Down the road.
He pushed the gas-knob to the floor;
Almost too late
Right in the front of him he saw
A gray wall rising with a narrow gate.
This was a section of his state
That Wild Bill
Had not seen before.
His car leapt towards it with a roar.

His hubcaps grazed
The big black gate;
He slowed the wheel,
The old V 8
Missed by a hair
A big black mastiff lying there.
Then he spied
A crowd ahead;
"It's my hips this time,"
Old Wild Bill said,
But he grabbed his brake,
Stopped on the dime;
The engine sputtered,
Shuddered,
Stuttered,
Died with a groan, a cough, and a shake.
Wild Bill looked
But he could not speak;
What he saw there
Left him weak.

Coming toward
His dead machine
Was the worst looking mob
He had ever seen.
Then he heard such
An ungodly yell,
He knew
At last
He had gone to Hell.

Wild Bill said,
"I will be damn.
Been asked here frequent,
And here I am."

The devils rushed at him
In a swarm,
And the cool
Wild Bill
Grew awful warm.
It looked like he'd
Broke up a meeting;
But this was the Convocation's
Greeting:
They climbed all over
His running board,
"Wild Bill, Wild Bill!"
Their shouting roared
And rang through all the streets of Hell:

"Give us the number,
Wild Bill,
Tell us
What fell!"

He Was a Man

It wasn't about no woman,
  It wasn't about no rape,
He wasn't crazy, and he wasn't drunk,
  An' it wasn't no shooting scrape,
    He was a man, and they laid him down.

He wasn't no quarrelsome feller,
  And he let other folks alone,
But he took a life, as a man will do,
  In a fight for to save his own,
    He was a man, and they laid him down.

He worked on his little homeplace
  Down on the Eastern Shore;
He had his family, and he had his friends,
  And he didn't expect much more,
    He was a man, and they laid him down.

He wasn't nobody's great man,
  He wasn't nobody's good,
Was a po' boy tried to get from life
  What happiness he could,
    He was a man, and they laid him down.

He didn't abuse Tom Wickley,
  Said nothing when the white man curst,
But when Tom grabbed his gun, he pulled his own,
  And his bullet got there first,
    He was a man, and they laid him down.

Didn't catch him in no manhunt,
  But they took him from a hospital bed,
Stretched on his back in the nigger ward,
  With a bullet wound in his head,
    He was a man, and they laid him down.

It didn't come off at midnight
  Nor yet at the break of day,
It was in the broad noon daylight,

When they put po' Will away,
    He was a man, and they laid him down.

Didn't take him to no swampland,
    Didn't take him to no woods,
Didn't hide themselves, didn't have no masks,
    Didn't wear no Ku Klux hoods,
        He was a man, and they laid him down.

They strung him up on Main Street,
    On a tree in the Court House Square,
And people came from miles around
    To enjoy a holiday there,
        He was a man, and they laid him down.

They hung him and they shot him,
    They piled packing cases around,
They burnt up Will's black body,
    'Cause he shot a white man down;
        "He was a man, and we'll lay him down."

It wasn't no solemn business,
    Was more like a barbecue,
The crackers yelled when the fire blazed,
    And the women and the children too—
        "He was a man, and we laid him down."

The Coroner and the Sheriff
    Said "Death by Hands Unknown."
The mob broke up by midnight,
    "Another uppity Nigger gone—
        He was a man, an' we laid him down."

Elder Mistletoe

Now Elder Johnson's name been changed
  To Elder Mistletoe;
And if you wants to hear it, here's
  De way de story go.

    Now Elder had a hard time
      Keeping his churchfolks straight,
    Funerals was too early,
      And marriages too late.

Like Job he was long patienced
  But when he was alone
Said, "Lawd, I been rebuked and scorned,
  But still, thy will be done."

    One time he told a Deacon
      To go a leetle slow;
    De Deacon and his fellow crooks
      Decided he must go.

And since de Elder's salary
  Was forty months behind,
De deacons board—it passed de vote
  To pay him off in kind.

    And fo' de four long wearying years
      Dat he had served de cause
    Dey piled a table full of stuff
      And dis was what it was:

A dominicker rooster,
  And a white leghorn hen,
Had been upon ole Noah's ark,
  And both had whiskers then.

    Two pounds of dried up spare-ribs,
      Some hogshead and some chine,
    A coupla quarts of black eyed peas,
      And a jug of homemade wine.

Was good enough for picklin'
  And a bucket full of lard
And a peck of arsh potatoes
  Was leetle, and was hard.

     And Elder looked down on de pile
       Of stuff upon de flo'
     And de look he had upon his face
       Was not like Job's no mo'!

"De time has come, dear brethren,
  When good friends has to part,
So let us sing 'O What a Change
  Don Took Place in My Heart.'"

     De song was done, the folks was sharp
       To see what thing was next
     Den Elder cast his eyes on high
       An' slowly took his text.

"Now blessed be de meek," he said,
  "For, lo, they shall inherit
All of de good things of de yearth,
  Least ways in de sperrit.

     "Been wid you, lo, dise many years
       In de vineyard all alone,
     Was never de first nor yet de last
       To throw de accusin' stone.

"You been mo' dan particular
  'Bout how yo' pastor live,
De house you gave him warn't no house,
  It was a first class sieve.

     "De salary you promised me,
       Got helt up on de way,
     But how you holds me in yo' heart
       I sho' kin see today.

"And fo' de family of my church
  Done prayed down on my knees

But I naver looked at all, at all
    Fo' offerins lak dese.

      "Bretheren, sistern, it is not fair
        For me to be de one
      To reap all of de good things
        Now yo' harvestin' is done.

"It is not right dat I should take
    De bounty of your toil,
When yo' victrolas ain't all paid for,
    And yo' cars need gas and oil.

      "I know jes' what de good book say
        An' jes what it allows
      But I ought not take dis food you brought
        When you could give it to yo' sows."

Den he turned to leave de rostrum
    And on his coat below
Tied wid a little red ribbon,
    Was a sprig of mistletoe.

Crispus Attucks McKoy

I sing of a hero,
Unsung, unrecorded,
Known by the name
Of Crispus Attucks McKoy,
Born, bred in Boston,
Stepson of Garvey,
Cousin of Trotter,
Godson of Du Bois.

No monastic hairshirt
Stung flesh more bitterly
Than the white coat
In which he was arrayed;
But what was his agony
On entering the drawing-room
To hear a white woman
Say slowly, "One spade."

He threw up his job,
His scorn was sublime,
And he left the bridge party
Simply aghast;
Lo, see him striding
Out of the front door
A free man again
His infamy past.

Down at the Common,
The cradle of freedom,
Another shock nearly
Carried him away
Someone called out "Shine"
And he let loose a blue streak,
And the poor little bootblack
Slunk frightened away.

In a bakery window
He read with a glance
"Brown Betties for sale"
And his molars gnashed;

Up came the kerbstone,
Back went his trusty arm,
Swift was his gesture,
The plate glass was smashed.

On the sub, Crispus
Could have committed murder,
Mayhem and cannibalism,
When he heard a maid
Say to the cherub
Opposite to her,
"Come over here, darling,
Here's a little shade."

But down at the Gardens,
He knew was his refuge,
Recompense for insults,
Solace for grief,
A Negro battler,
Slugging Joe Johnson
Was fighting an Irishman
Battling Dan O'Keefe.

The garden was crammed,
Mickeys, Kikes, Bohunks,
Polacks and Dagoes,
All over the place,
Crispus strode in,
Regally, boldly,
The sole representative
Of his race.

The fight was even,
When Joey hit Dan,
The heart of Crispus
Shone with a steady glow,
When Dan hit Joey,
Crispus groaned "foul,"
"Oh the dirty low-down
So-and-so."

In the tenth round,
Dan got to swinging,

Joey was dazed,
And clinched and held,
When suddenly,
Right behind Crispus,
"Kill the Nigger!"
Somebody yelled.

Crispus got up
In all of his fury;
Lightning bolts zigzagged
Out of his eyes,
With a voice like thunder
He blurted his challenge,
"Will the bastard who said that
Please arise."

Thirty-five thousand
Nordics and Alpines,
Hebrews and Gentiles,
As one man arose,
See how our hero,
Armed with his noble cause,
Armored with righteousness
To battle goes.

They found an ankle in Dedham,
A thighbone in Maldon,
An elbow in Somerville,
Both nostrils in Lynn,
And on Boston Common
Lay one of his eyebrows,
The cap of his knee,
And a piece of his shin.

Peabody Museum
Has one of his eardrums;
His sound heart was found
In Lexington;
But over the reaches
From Cape Cod to Frisco
The soul of our hero
Goes marching on . . .

A Bad, Bad Man

Forget about your Jesse James,
  And Billy the Kid;
I'll tell you instead what
  A black boy did.

    John Bias was a squinchy runt,
      Four foot two,
    Married to a strapping broad.
      Big-legged Sue.

Another boy, Sam Johnson,
  Was getting lynched because
His black mule had bust
  A white man's jaws.

    The crackers gathered in the woods
      Early that night.
    Corn liquor in pop bottles
      Got 'em right.

They tied Sam Johnson to a tree.
  Threw liquor on the fire.
Like coal oil it made the flames
  Shoot higher.

    Then Johnny Bias rushed in
      Looking awful sore,
    Waving a great big
      Forty-four.

The doctor he fell sick,
  The preacher fell on his knees,
The kids fell bass ackwards
  From the trees.

    And all the women scattered
      Right close behind the men;
    Then brave Little Johnnie walked
      Out again.

The fire had burnt the ropes;
  Sam jumped up and was gone
Down the other road from what
  The mob was on.

    The state troops cam a-troopin'
      Three days later,
    And stayed near twenty minutes to
      Investigate.

The crackers spoke, from then on,
  Of the giant nigger,
Every day he grew a
  Little bigger.

    Johnnie was told the next day
      What he had done for Sam,
    Scratched his head and said, "Well
      I be dam!

"Never had no notion
  To save nobody's life,
I was only jes a-lookin'
  For my wife."

Break of Day

Big Jess fired on the Alabama Central,
Man in full, babe, man in full.
Been throwing on coal for Mister Murphy
From times way back, baby, times way back.

Big Jess had a pleasing woman, name of Mamie,
Sweet-hipted Mama, sweet-hipted Mame;
Had a boy growing up for to be a fireman,
Just like his pa, baby, like his pa.

Out by the roundhouse Jess had his cabin,
Longside the tracks, babe, long the tracks,
Jess pulled the whistle when they high-balled past it
"I'm on my way, baby, on my way."

Crackers craved the job what Jess was holding,
Times right tough, babe, times right tough,
Warned Jess to quit his job for a white man,
Jess he laughed, baby, he jes' laughed.

He picked up his lunch-box, kissed his sweet woman,
Sweet-hipted Mama, sweet-hipted Mame,
His son walked with him to the white-washed palings,
"Be seeing you soon, son, see you soon."

Mister Murphy let Big Jess talk on the whistle
"So long sugar baby, so long babe";
Train due back in the early morning
Breakfast time, baby, breakfast time.

Mob stopped the train crossing Black Bear Mountain
Shot rang out, babe, shot rang out.
They left Big Jess on the Black Bear Mountain,
Break of day, baby, break of day.

Sweet Mame sits rocking, waiting for the whistle
Long past due, babe, long past due.
The grits are cold, and the coffee's boiled over,
But Jess done gone, baby he done gone.

Rent Day Blues

I says to my baby
"Baby, but de rent is due;
Can't noways figger
What we ever gonna do."

My baby says, "Honey,
Dontcha worry 'bout de rent.
Looky here, daddy,
At de money what de good Lord sent."

Says to my baby,
"Baby, I been all aroun';
Never knowed de good Lord
To send no greenbacks down."

Baby says, "Dontcha
Bother none about de Lord;
Thing what I'm figgerin'
Is how to get de next month's board."

Says to my baby,
"I'd best get me on a spell;
Get your rent from heaven,
Maybe get your food from hell."

Baby says, "One old
Miracle I never see,
Dat a man lak you
Can ever get away from me."

I says, "Ain't no magician,
Baby, dat's a sho-Gawd fact;
But jest you watch me
Do de disappearin' act."

"Ef you do, you're better
Dan de devil or de Lord on high";
An' I stayed wid my baby
Fo' a devilish good reason why.

The Ballad of Joe Meek

I

You cain't never tell
  How far a frog will jump,
When you jes' see him planted
  On his big broad rump.

      Nor what a monkey's thinking
        By the working of his jaws—
      You jes' cain't figger;
        And I knows, because

Had me a buddy,
  Soft as pie
Joe Meek they called him
  And they didn't lie.

      The good book say
        "Turn the other cheek,"
      But that warn't no turning
        To my boy Joe Meek.

He turned up all parts,
  And baigged you to spank,
Pulled down his breeches,
  And supplied the plank.

      The worm that didn't turn
        Was a rattlesnake to Joe:
      Wasn't scary—jes' meek, suh,
        Was made up so.

II

It was late in August
  What dey calls dog days,
Made even beetle hounds
  Git bulldog ways.

Would make a pet bunny
  Chase a bad blood-hound
Make a new-born baby
  Slap his grandpa down.

The air it was muggy
  And heavy with heat,
The people all sizzled
  Like frying meat.

  The icehouse was heaven
    The pavements was hell
  Even Joe didn't feel
    So agreeable.

Strolling down Claiborne
  In the wrong end of town
Joe saw two policemen
  Knock a po' gal down.

  He didn't know her at all,
    Never saw her befo',
  But that didn't make no difference,
    To my ole boy Joe.

Walks up to the cops,
  And, very polite,
Ast them ef they thought
  They had done *just right.*

  One cracked him with his billy
    Above the left eye,
  One thugged him with his pistol
    And let him lie.

  III

When he woke up, and knew
  What the cops had done,
Went to a hockshop,
  Got hisself a gun.

Felt mo' out of sorts
   Than ever befo',
So he went on a rampage
   My ole boy Joe.

Shot his way to the station house.
   Rushed right in,
Wasn't nothing but space
   Where the cops had been.

      They called the reserves,
         And the national guard,
      Joe was in a cell
         Overlooking the yard.

The machine guns sputtered,
   Didn't faze Joe at all—
But evvytime he fired
   A cop would fall.

      The tear-gas made him laugh
         When they let it fly,
      Laughing gas made him hang
         His head an' cry.

He threw the hand grenades back
   With a outshoot drop,
An' evvytime he threw
   They was one less cop.

      The Chief of Police said
         "What kinda *man* is this?"
      And held up his shirt
         For a armistice.

"Stop gunning, black boy,
   And we'll let you go."
"I thank you very kindly,"
   Said my ole boy Joe.

      "We promise you safety
         If you'll leave us be—"

Joe said: "That's agreeable
    Sir, by me . . ."

IV

The sun had gone down
    The air it was cool,
Joe stepped out on the pavement
    A fighting foól.

        Had walked from the jail
            About half a square,
        When a cop behind a post
            Let him have it fair.

Put a bullet in his left side
    And one in his thigh,
But Joe didn't lose
    His shootin' eye.

        Drew a cool bead
            On the cop's broad head;
        "I returns you yo' favor"
            And the cop fell dead.

The next to last words
    He was heard to speak,
Was just what you would look for
    From my boy Joe Meek.

        Spoke real polite
            To the folks standing by:
        "Would you please do me one kindness,
            Fo' I die?

"Won't be here much longer
    To bother you so,
Would you bring me a drink of water
    Fo' I go?"

The very last words
  He was heard to say,
Showed a different Joe talking
  In a different way.

"Ef my bullets weren't gone,
  An' my strength all spent—
I'd send the chief something
  With a compliment.

    "And we'd race to hell,
      And I'd best him there,
    Like I would of done here
      Ef he'd played me fair."

    V

So you cain't never tell
  How fas' a dog can run
When you see him a-sleeping,
  In the sun.

NO HIDING PLACE

Went down to the rocks to hide my face,
The rocks cried out no hiding place.

to
Michael Harper, recoverer
Michael Winston, restorer
Michael Campbell, godson
Sterling Stuckey, renewer
Sterling Jenkins, godson

Part One
HARLEM STOPOVER

Harlem Happiness

I think there is in this the stuff for many lyrics:—
A dago fruit stand at three A.M.; the wop asleep, his woman
Knitting a tiny garment, laughing when we approached her,
Flashing a smile from white teeth, then weighing out the grapes,
Grapes large as plums, and tart and sweet as—well we know the lady
And purplish red and firm, quite as this lady's lips are. . . .
We laughed, all three when she awoke her swarthy, snoring Pietro
To make us change, which we, rich paupers, left to help the garment.
We swaggered off; while they two stared, and laughed in understanding,
And thanked us lovers who brought back an old Etrurian springtide.
Then, once beyond their light, a step beyond their pearly smiling
We tasted grapes and tasted lips, and laughed at sleepy Harlem,

And when the huge Mick cop stomped by, a'swingin' of his billy
You nodded to him gaily, and I kissed you with him looking,
Beneath the swinging light that weakly fought against the mist
That settled on Eighth Avenue, and curled around the houses.
And he grinned too and understood the wisdom of our madness.
That night at least the world was ours to spend, nor were we misers.
Ah, Morningside with Maytime awhispering in the foliage!
Alone, atop the city,—the tramps were still in shelter—
And moralizing lights that peered up from the murky distance
Seemed soft as our two cigarette ends burning slowly, dimly,
And careless as the jade stars that winked upon our gladness. . . .

And when I flicked my cigarette, and we watched it falling, falling,
It seemed a shooting meteor, that we, most proud creators
Sent down in gay capriciousness upon a trivial Harlem—

And then I madly quoted lyrics from old kindred masters,
Who wrote of you, unknowing you, for far more lucky me—
And you sang broken bits of song, and we both slept in snatches,
And so the night sped on too swift, with grapes, and words and kisses,
And numberless cigarette ends glowing in the darkness
Old Harlem slept regardless, but a motherly old moon—
Shone down benevolently on two happy wastrel lovers. . . .

Negro Improvement League

I wondered at the huge blockade
At the ridiculous parade
That limped along in the straitlaced coats
And Sunday shoes too tight—

Old men and women comfortless
Would curse dearbought impressiveness
And Seventh Avenue's scorching heat,
In stuffy flats, that night

I knew, and so, I puzzled out
Just what the fuss was all about
Just why the noise and feathers, and
Regalia absurd

And what new dreams could now convoke
My gullible and naive folk
To strut their stuff so painfully
Until at Thirty Third

I quickly understood the why—
For there, most startling, not my eye
A most sufficient reason—an
Achievement of the race—

For who was there but Gwendolyn
With a frock she looked quite stunning in
And a brand new hat, near worthy of
Her impudent brown face

Her roguish shoulders, and her neat
And pretty legs, and naughty feet
In patent leather slippers, all
Were really quite too bad

Progressive Ethiopians,
Societies for Race Advance,
Should go down on their knees, and thank
Her mother and her dad.

The Temple

The orator finished his eulogy,
  A voice rang through the hall,
"Would you mind if I ahkst a few queshuns?"
  "My dear mohn, not at all."

"War die Marrcus Garrvey a gretter mohn
  Dan General George Washingtum war?"
"Why certainly, mohn, assuredly, mohn,
  A greater mohn by far."

"Well what about Booker Washington,
  Have Marrcus got him beat?"
"Why, mohn, what have de Booker done
  To equal de *Blahck Star Fleet?*"

"War he gretter dan Abraham Lincoln
  What set de niggruhs free?"
"Oi yes, mohn, Marcus have done more,
  Marcus are greater than he."

"War he gretter mohn dan Pershing
  De mohn what won de war?"
"Oi yes mohn, Marcus Garvey
  He have accumplished more."

"War he greater dan Herbert Hoover
  De prasident of dese stet'?"
"Oi, mohn, don't be de bressed fool,
  Hoover he not so gret."

"Well, one mo' queshun I like to ahks
  An' den I shall be done;
Ar he de gretter mohn dan Jesus Christ
  Who die for every wan?"

The crowd was breathless; the orator's brow
  Beaded with honest sweat,
"Well . . . Oi, mohn, give de faller little chahnce
  He de very young mohn yet. . . ."

Roberta Lee

A Lee of Leesburg in this place.
Surely the gray ghost of her father's father
Would toss in his dark grave, and set the medals
Jingling upon the Confederate chest, still arched.
She, Roberta Lee, in this hell-hole of the North
A Harlem cabaret, logical outcome of Appomattox
She gestured for another drink of gin,
Bar sinister relative, for damyanks and niggers,
Of bourbon in tall glasses, frosty and delicate,
Crowned with a sprig of mint.
Roberta!
She hated all of this, and took another drink.
But though her mind grew cloudy, her eyes were fiercer
Probing the murk to fix the devilishness.
Twelve undraped maenads, some nearly as white as she,
Some even blonde, the darkest a rose-brown,
Whipped into contortions, lithely provocative,
Tap-danced, pirouetted, whirled through a skilled routine.
"The hussies," thought Roberta, and gulped down the raw gin
One danced beside her table with abandon,
Upon her plump firm thigh a mole; within
Her sparkling eyes a daring and a surety.
Henry applauded, beamed, showed the world he liked it.
"And he from Texas, too," Roberta thought.
Then wearily, "Perhaps that is the reason."
Suddenly, she turned to the dancing girl,
"Get away," she whispered, and her mind
Concerned with Texas Henry, filled with sickly fear,
Remembering; her bitter eyes spoke more: "You sassy wench
You lewd and impudent nigger, get the hell away."
But to the rose of Dixie, to Roberta, Southerner,
The chorine presented, due South, a Southern exposure.
Roberta shuddered. How she hated it all:
The elaborate hangings, the sensuous decorations
The reek of cigarette smoke, perfume, and liquor,
The oily Jew who introduced the 'artists',
The bold glances of the sleek boys in the band,
Of a group of Negroes grouped in a far corner,
Even their quiet was to be resented—
"They seem like dark cats ready for a spring"

But most she was revolted at the girls,
Proud of their beauty, decked out in fetching costumes,
Now in neat bandanas and blue ginghams
Quickly pulled above their shapely knees,
Now in silk shorts and jeweled brassieres,
"Disgusting immorality," thought Roberta,
And wondered if Texas Henry would like them better than her.
"I always heard that they could love," she mused.
"I hate them, oh, I hate them," she cried aloud
"Hate who?" "Oh, give me another drink"
She drank and coughed.
"Oh less go home; don't wanta see any mo."
Then he appeared.
Ape-like in body, with his long arms dangling,
Nearly to his feet resembling flatboats,
Upon his head a crazy hat, his face
A black mask, except for large white circles
About his eyes, and thickly painted lips.
He danced.
She drank some more to wake her to attention.
He shuffled his flat feet, swing back and fro,
Grotesque, ridiculous; he could not keep his balance,
His lips got in his way, he fell to the slippery floor,
While the drummer struck *zip, boom,* to time his falling.
He arched over backwards, fell upon his head,
Boom went the drum, bang went the cymbals,
"Oh isn't that lovely," breathed Roberta.
"That's the kind of nigger I know," said Roberta,
Too rapt to hear Texas Henry's "Oh yeah?"
And she remembered all she had heard
Her grandfather declaim of the golden age,
"The niggruh," he had said, "is the most comical animal"
The clown fell over himself a few more times.
Bent over backwards to pick up his handkerchief
Between his teeth; half rose, half fell; Roberta tittered;
Then he fell *bang, bang,* somersaulted, crept off,
Gorilla like, with stupid mask impassive
Applause rose to the low-ceiling, round on round.
He made one bow, then disappeared for good.
Roberta Lee was frantic.
"Oh bring him back," she whimpered.
"Please bring him back again."

Real Mammy Song

*(With proudful apologies to Irving Berlin et al.
and all the Tin Pan Alley Manipulators)*

Mammy
Sun shines east, sun shines west,
Moon shines on de boy
    She loved de best
    Cowering in the canebrake
Down in the canebrake
Close by de mill
Dere lies a culluhd boy
    Terrified and still
Lordy how he played it
Lordy how he swayed it
An' they called him Sunny Jim
    Five bullets for crackers
    And the last for him
Number one for the Sheriff
Number two for the bum
Three more to make ready
And here they come
Rich man, poor man
Beggar
Bootlegger
View halloo
And here they come
I'm coming, Virginia
    And the last for Sunny Jim
Oh, tuck him to sleep
In his old Kentucky home
Far, far away
Where the Carolina moon is shining
Shining
And the darkies all are
Gay.

    They done took
    Poor Jim away. . . .

    They done took
    My son away. . . .

The Law for George

(Curriculum For Dr. Hancock's School)
Sociology 143; Tort 23

George:
Don't be no Chinaman
Let me get you told
For once

PORTER

Take her tray
Into her Pullman compartment
She may be in morning all-shabby
Take her gin and gingerale
She may be in cool of the evening lingerie
That's all right
You got your white coat on, ain't you?
Okeh.
But don't ever ride
With her in a Pullman
Without that white coat on
Don't even buy
No ticket for a Pullman
She might just be thinking 'bout riding
You fool you
You want to make the lady paint?

COOK

Cook her food for her
Season it, taste it,
But don't sit in the same room
Eating with her
You want to poison her, you fool?

REDCAP

Carry her bags for her
Listen to her kiddin'
Laugh with her

But don't never offer
To help her with no bundles
When you ain't got
Yo' redcap on.
See?

HOUSEMAN

In your overhalls
Leaning on yo' rake
Talk to her long as she wants
Cut roses for her
Give her a bouquet
Go all through the house
Putting things to right
Okeh.
But don't be no Chinaman, George.
Don't never put on
No collar and no tie
Don't never hand her no flower
Without those overhalls on.
See?

CHAUFFEUR

Drive her car wherever
The notion takes her
In traffic, on the turnpike
Through narrow country lanes
Day or night.
Okeh.
But don't walk behind her
On no state highway
In the broadest of broad daylight.
You ain't so ignorant
I gotta tell you that?
Heh?

HARTSHORN

When the master calls you
Young master, old master,
Go in his room
And do his bidding
Remember your manners, child.
He'll explain race purity
And other deep subjects
Economics of amalgamation
The truth about reconstruction.

When you go out
Make your courtesy
Say "Thank you, sir."

(And don't never let him catch you
Whisperin' to George)

The New Congo

Suave big jigs in a conference room,
Big job jigs, with their jobs unstable,
Sweated and fumed and trembled 'round the table
Trembled 'round the table
Sat around as gloomy as the watchers of a tomb
Tapped upon the table
Boom, Boom, Boom.
With their soft pigs' knuckles and their fingers and their thumbs
In a holy sweat that their time had come
Boomlay, boomlay, boomlay, boom.
How can I go back to being a bum.
Then I had religion, then I had a vision
I could not turn from their anguish in derision.
Then I saw the Uncle Tom, creeping through the black
Cutting through the bigwoods with his trousers slack
With hinges on his knees, and with putty up his back.
Then along the line from the big wig jigs
Then I heard the plaint of the money-lust song.
And the cry for status yodeled loud and long
And a line of argument loud and wrong
And "Bucks" screamed the trombones and the flutes of the spokesmen
"Bucks" screamed the newly made Ph.D. Doctors
Utilize the sure-fire goofie dust powder
Garner the shekels
Encompass mazuma
Boomlay, boomlay, boomlay, booma.
Bing.
Tremolo, mendicant implorations
From the mouths of Uncle Toms
To the great foundations.
"Jack is a good thing
A goddamn good thing
The only bad thing
Is there ain't enough.
Boom, fool the whitefolks
Boom, gyp the jigaboos
Boom, get the prestige

Strut your stuff."
Listen to the cry of the Negro mass
Down to its uppers, down on its ass.
Hear how the big jigs fool 'em still
With their services paid from the white man's till.
Listen to the cunning exhortations
Wafted to the ears of the big foundations
Blown to the big white boss paymasters
Faint hints of far-reaching grim disasters.
"Be careful what you do
Or your Mumbo-jumbo stuff for Sambo
And all of the other
Bilge for Sambo
Your Mumbo-Jumbo will get away from you.
Your Bimbo-Sambo will revolt from you.
Better let Uncle Tombo see it through,
A little long green at this time will do. . . ."

Part Two
THE COTTON SOUTH

Arkansas Chant

The devil is a rider
In slouch hat and boots,
Gun by his side,
Bull whip in his hand,
The devil is a rider;
The rider is a devil
Riding his buck stallion
Over the land.

The poor-white and nigger sinners
Are low-down in the valley,
The rider is a devil

And there's hell to pay;
The devil is a rider,
God may be the owner,
But he's rich and forgetful,
And far away.

The Young Ones

With cotton to the doorstep
No place to play;
No time: what with chopping cotton
All the day.

In the broken down car
They jounce up and down
Pretend to be steering
On the way to town.

It's as far as they'll get
For many a year;
Cotton brought them
And will keep them here.

The spare-ribbed yard dog
Has gone away;
The kids, just as hungry,
Have to stay.

In the two-roomed shack
Their mammy is lying,
With a little new brother
On her arm, crying.

Another mouth to feed
Another body to bed,
Another to grow up
Underfed.

But their pappy's happy
And they hear him say:
"The good Lord giveth,
And taketh away.

"It's two more hands
For to carry a row;
Praise God from whom
All blessings flow."

Old Lem

I talked to old Lem
and old Lem said:
  "They weigh the cotton
  They store the corn
    We only good enough
    To work the rows;
  They run the commissary
  They keep the books
    We gotta be grateful
    For being cheated;
  Whippersnapper clerks
  Call us out of our name
    We got to say mister
    To spindling boys
  They make our figgers
  Turn somersets
  We buck in the middle
    Say, "Thankyuh, sah."
    They don't come by ones
    They don't come by twos
    But they come by tens.

  "They got the judges
  They got the lawyers
  They got the jury-rolls
  They got the law
    They don't come by ones
  They got the sheriffs
  They got the deputies
     They don't come by twos
  They got the shotguns
  They got the rope
    We git the justice
    In the end
     And they come by tens.

  "Their fists stay closed
  Their eyes look straight
    Our hands stay open
    Our eyes must fall

They don't come by ones
They got the manhood
They got the courage
They don't come by twos
We got to slink around
Hangtailed hounds.
They burn us when we dogs
They burn us whem we men
They come by tens . . .

"I had a buddy
Six foot of man
Muscled up perfect
Game to the heart
They don't come by ones
Outworked and outfought
Any man or two men
They don't come by twos
He spoke out of turn
At the commissary
They gave him a day
To git out the county
He didn't take it.
He said 'Come and get me.'
They came and got him
And they came by tens.
He stayed in the county—
He lays there dead.

They don't come by ones
They don't come by twos
But they come by tens."

Sharecroppers

When they rode up at first dark and called his name,
He came out like a man from his little shack.
He saw his landlord, and he saw the sheriff,
And some well-armed riff-raff in the pack.
When they fired questions about the meeting,
He stood like a man gone deaf and dumb,
But when the leaders left their saddles,
He knew then that his time had come.
In the light of the lanterns the long cuts fell,
And his wife's weak moans and the children's wails
Mixed with the sobs he could not hold.
But he wouldn't tell, he would not tell.
The Union was his friend, and he was Union,
And there was nothing a man could say.
So they trussed him up with stout ploughlines,
Hitched up a mule, dragged him far away
Into the dark woods that tell no tales,
Where he kept his secrets as well as they.

He would not give away the place,
Nor who they were, neither white nor black,
Nor tell what his brothers were about.
They lashed him, and they clubbed his head;
One time he parted his bloody lips
Out of great pain and greater pride,
One time, to laugh in his landlord's face;
Then his landlord shot him in the side.
He toppled, and the blood gushed out.
But he didn't mumble ever a word,
And cursing, they left him there for dead.
He lay waiting quiet, until he heard
The growls and the mutters dwindle away;
"Didn't tell a single thing," he said,
Then to the dark woods and the moon
He gave up one secret before he died:
"We gonna clean out dis brushwood round here soon,
Plant de white-oak and de black-oak side by side."

Master and Man

The yellow ears are crammed in Mr. Cromartie's bin
The wheat is tight sacked in Mr. Cromartie's barn.
The timothy is stuffed in Mr. Cromartie's loft.
The ploughs are lined up in Mr. Cromartie's shed.
The cotton has gone to Mr. Cromartie's factor.
The money is in Mr. Cromartie's bank.
Mr. Cromartie's son made his frat at the college.
Mr. Cromartie's daughter has got her new car.
The veranda is old, but the fireplace is rosy.
Well done, Mr. Cromartie. Time now for rest.

Blackened sticks line the furrows that Uncle Ned laid.
Bits of fluff are in the corners where Uncle Ned ginned.
The mules he ploughed are sleek in Mr. Cromartie's pastures.
The hoes grow dull in Mr. Cromartie's shed.
His winter rations wait on the commissary shelves;
Mr. Cromartie's ledger is there for his service.
Uncle Ned daubs some mortar between the old logs.
His children have traipsed off to God knows where.
His old lady sits patching the old, thin denims;
She's got a new dress, and his young one a doll,
He's got five dollars. The year has come round.
The harvest is over: Uncle Ned's harvesting,
Mr. Cromartie's harvest. Time now for rest.

Part Three
DOWN IN ATLANTA

Southern Cop

Let us forgive Ty Kendricks.
The place was Darktown. He was young.
His nerves were jittery. The day was hot.
The Negro ran out of the alley.
And so he shot.

Let us understand Ty Kendricks.
The Negro must have been dangerous,
Because he ran;
And here was a rookie with a chance
To prove himself a man.

Let us condone Ty Kendricks
If we cannot decorate.
When he found what the Negro was running for,
It was too late;
And all we can say for the Negro is
It was unfortunate.

Let us pity Ty Kendricks,
He has been through enough,
Standing there, his big gun smoking,
Rabbit-scared, alone,
Having to hear the wenches wail
And the dying Negro moan.

Mr. Danny

Oh, Danny got a goat to ride,
Oh, Danny got a goat to ride,
He ain't had nothing,
Won't never have anything,
But Danny is satisfied.

Dirty as sin, an' hookworms
Pluggin' away inside,
Bats in his belfry flappin' round,
But he got a black goat to ride.

Cockleburred and amber stained,
Neck red as a clay hillside,
Smells as loud as a stableyard,
Still Danny got a goat to ride.

With his "Nigger this" and his "Black Coon that"
"Bigard, I'll beat yo' stinkin' hide!"
Danny feels equal to a natural king:
Mister Danny got a goat to ride.

An Old Woman Remembers

Her eyes were gentle, her voice was for soft singing
In the stiff-backed pew, or on the porch when evening
Comes slowly over Atlanta. But she remembered.
She said: "After they cleaned out the saloons and the dives
The drunks and the loafers, they thought that they had better
Clean out the rest of us. And it was awful.
They snatched men off of street-cars, beat up women.
Some of our men fought back and killed too. Still
It wasn't their habit. And then the orders came
For the milishy, and the mob went home,
And dressed up in their soldiers' uniforms,
And rushed back shooting just as wild as ever.
Some leaders told us to keep faith in the law,
In the governor; some did not keep that faith,
Some never had it; he was white, too and the time
Was near election, and the rebs were mad.
He wasn't stopping hornets with his head bare.
The white folks at the big houses, some of them
Kept all their servants home under protection
But that was all the trouble they could stand.
And some were put out when their cooks and yard-boys
Were thrown from cars and beaten, and came late or not at all.
And the police they helped the mob, and the milishy
They helped the police. And it got worse and worse.

"They broke into groceries, drug-stores, barber-shops,
It made no difference whether white or black.
They beat a lame bootblack until he died,
They cut an old man open with jack-knives
The newspapers named us black brutes and mad dogs.
So they used a gun butt on the president
Of our seminary where a lot of folks
Had set up praying prayers the whole night through.
And then," she said, "our folks got sick and tired
Of being chased and beaten and shot down.
All of a sudden, one day, they all got sick and tired
The servants they put down their mops and pans
And brooms and hoes and rakes and coachman whips,
Bad niggers stopped their drinking Dago red,
Good Negroes figured they had prayed enough,

All came back home—they had been too long away—
A lot of visitors had been looking for them.
They sat on their front stoops and in their yards,
Not talking much, but ready; their welcome ready:
Their shotguns oiled and loaded on their knees.

"And then
There wasn't any riot any more."

Transfer

I

It must have been that the fellow was tongue-tied,
Or absent-minded, or daft with the heat,
But howsoeverbeit he didn't say sir,
So they took and bounced him out on the street.

And then the motorman brained him with his crank,
And the conductor clubbed him with his ₒun,
But before they could place the nickels on his eyes,
The cops rushed up to see justice done.

The city-court judge was merciful to him:
Gave him just four years and suspended his fine,
For bruising white knuckles, inciting to riot,
And holding up traffic on the Peachtree line.

When the boy came to, he was still right skittish,
They figured they had got him rid of his harm,
By beating his head, and displacing his jawbone,
So they made him a trusty on the prison-farm.

II

But one day a red sun beat on the red hills
As he was in the pasture, haltering a mare,
And something went snap in his trusty old head
And he started a-riding away from there.

When he got to Atlanta, the folks took him in,
And fed him and clothed him, and hid him away;
And let him out only when the cops disappear
From the streets of Darktown at the dusk of day:

Then he goes to the car-stop and takes his stand,
And some call him daffy, and some call him smart,
But all have heard the one text he's been preaching,
And some have the whole sermon down by heart:

"I stayed in my place, and my place stayed wid me,
Took what was dished, said I liked it fine:
Figgered they would see that I warn't no trouble,
Figgered this must be the onliest line.

"But this is the wrong line we been ridin',
This route doan git us where we got to go.
Got to git transferred to a new direction.
We can stand so much, then doan stan no mo'."

Episode

Black Joe Harmon has lost his job.
The last hunk of bread went into his lunchbox
This morning; eight dollars of the final pay-slip
Belong already to the rent-collector,
A buck and a-half must last him until. . . .
Maybe, forever. . . .
His mouth is dry; fear throttles his brain.
Homeward he shuffles, unaware, lost.
Maybe, maybe, forever . . . maybe, not ever no more.
At Jefferson and Park,
He lumbers across on the amber switch.
The gasping of brakes, the shrieking of wheels
Wake him, drag him out of the black wilderness.
"Gawdamnit, naygur, watch where yuh going!"
"Naygur, naygur," say the voices, the glaring eyes.
Backing off from the trolley, his strong frame quivering
He stops short again as the brakes of a car
Screech, and a bumper grazes his knee.
A roadster, three light-skinned Negroes in front,
A dude and his girl friend at play in the rumble:
"Scared yuh, hey, Sam? We'll git yuh next time"
"Sam, Sam"—Derision floated back to him.
Oh nothing left now, let him rush from his shame
Home to his alley, curse his dulled wife,
Cuff his baby, stamp, rage till exhausted
In the bare lamp-lighted coop called home.
Let him guzzle liquor, drink upon drink,
Raw flaming spirit of barely cooked corn
Let him stagger from the rickety stoop of his house,
Switch blade in his pocket, hate in his heart,
White lightning hate, scorching his brain.
Oh, for a face to smash into pulp,
For the world's wrong there, all crowded before him,
Oh for a throat to glut his fierce hatred.
Let him rush out, now, drunken and sick,
Find where he can a crashing appeasement,
Let madness have him, let murder be served.
Let the world totter;
Let the end come.

All Are Gay

The picture of content should be complete:
I sing the happy pickaninnies
Underneath the Georgia moon.

There should be laughing, tumbling,
Wild flinging about of thin arms and legs and bottoms.

       'Tis summer, the darkies are gay
They are: down on Decatur Street
Two kids climb cartons like Bojangles,
Tap, tap, ta-ta-tap-
Dancing for the pennies of the passers-by.

Let the picture be complete, with all of its fixings:
The jigs, the singing, and the ceaseless play,
The perpetual wide-mouthed smiles.

And: in the paved alleys behind the wealthy homes,
The foragers dart thin wrists in glittering garbage-pails,
Find heels of soggy bread, and unstripped chops,
Topping off the feast with rinds of grapefruit
Or rattlesnake melons snitched from market piles,
With practiced looks thrown swiftly over their shoulders
For their arch-enemies, the cops.

Underneath the Georgia moon . . .

       M' ole man is on de chaingang
       Muh mammy's on relief

Down at the Lincoln Theater, little Abe is set free again.
Hears music that gets deep down, into his soul.
"Callin' all cars, callin' all cars," and the prolonged hiss,
"Black Ace. Black Ace." And his thin voice screams
When the tommy guns drill, and the bodies fall,
Mow them down, mow them down, gangsters or G-men,
So long as the folks get killt, no difference at all,
So long as the rattling gun-fire plays little Abe his song.

And the only pleasure exceeding this
Will come when he gets hold of the pearl-handled gat
Waiting for him, ready, in Moe Epstein's.

Gonna be the Black Ace hisself before the time ain't
    long.

Outside the theater he stalks his pa'dner,
Creeps up behind him, cocks his thumb,
Rams his forefinger against his side.
"Stick 'em up, dam yuh," his treble whines.

The squeals and the flight
Are more than he looked for, his laughter peals,
He is just at the bursting point with delight.
"Black Ace. Stick 'em up, feller. . . . I'm the Black Ace."

Oh, to grow up soon, to the top of glory,
With a glistening furrow on his dark face,
Badge of his manhood, pass-key to fame.
"Before the time ain't long," he says.
"Lord, before the time ain't long."

        The young folks roll in the cabins on the floor

And in the narrow unlighted streets,
Behind the shrouding vines and lattices,
Up the black foul alleys, the unpaved roads,
Sallie Lou and Johnnie Mae play the spies,
Ready, giggling, for experiments, for their unformed
    bodies
To be roughly clasped, for little wild cries,
For words learned of their elders on display:
"Gonna get me a boy friend," Sallie Lou says;
"Got me a man already," brags Johnnie Mae.

This is the schooling ungrudged by the state.
Short in time, as usual, but fashioned to last.
The scholars are apt, and never play truant.
The stockade is waiting. . . . And they will not be late.

Before, before the time ain't very long.

In the stockade: "Little boy, how come you hyeah?"
"Little bitty gal, how old are you?"
"Well, I got hyeah, didn't I? Whatchu keer?"
"I'm goin' on twelve years old."

Say of them then: "Like Topsy, they just grew."

Part Four
"ROCKS CRIED OUT"

Legend

The old black man was stood on the block
The old white man looked into his mouth
The old white man held up his fingers
"I own you, nigger,"
Said the old white man.

The old black man drove his plough afield
From sun-come-up until sun-go-down,
His hut was leaky, and the food was scarce,
"I'm grateful for these favors,"
Said the old black man.

The old black man had a pretty wife
The old white man took her to his house
The wife came back with a half-white baby.
"I'm glad to be of service,"
Said the old black man.

The old black man heard talk of his freedom
The old black man saw his mates take flight
He rushed the news to his old white master
"I thought it best you know it,"
Said the old black man.

The old black man lost his half-white daughter
Down the river, and a son in the swamp.
The old black man lost his wife in the grave.
"I've still got my master,"
Said the old black man.

The old black man saw his son grow sturdy
Saw his eyes taking stock of the old white man
Heard him say things past all believing,
"You're on the road to ruin,"
Said the old black man.

The old black man was hung by his thumbs
To the smokehouse rafters while the old cat lashed
He rubbed salt and water upon the welts
"I must have deserved it,"
Said the old black man.

The young black man got to asking questions
Why corn and cotton were his own for working
But not his at all in the shocks and the bales.
"You're a fool blasphemer,"
Said the old black man.

The old black man had talk with his master
The old white man was near to a stroke
The young black man would not be grateful
"After all you've done for him,"
Said the old black man.

The old white man took his whip from the wall,
The old black man brought the trace-chains from the barn,
The two old men bared their old men's muscles,
"Let me whip him into reason,"
Said the old black man.

The young black man faced his old black father.
The young black man faced the old white man.
He straightened his shoulders, and threw back his head,
"I wish you both in hell,"
Said the young black man.

The young black man broke the whipstock to pieces,
The young black man cut the lash into bits.
Then chained the old men together with the traces,
"Your fine day is over,"
Said the young black man.

Bitter Fruit of the Tree

They said to my grandmother: "Please do not be bitter,"
When they sold her first-born and let the second die,
When they drove her husband till he took to the swamplands,
And brought him home bloody and beaten at last.
They told her, "It is better you should not be bitter,
Some must work and suffer so that we, who must, can live,
Forgiving is noble, you must not be heathen bitter;
These are your orders: you *are* not to be bitter."
And they left her shack for their porticoed house.

They said to my father: "Please do not be bitter,"
When he ploughed and planted a crop not his,
When he weatherstripped a house that he could not enter,
And stored away a harvest he could not enjoy.
They answered his questions: "It does not concern you,
It is not for you to know, it is past your understanding,
All you need know is: you must not be bitter."
And they laughed on their way to reckon the crop,
And my father walked over the wide garnered acres
Where a cutting wind warned him of the cold to come.

They said to my brother: "Please do not be bitter,
Is it not sad to see the old place go to ruin?
The eaves are sprung and the chimney tower is leaning,
The sills, joists, and columns are rotten in the core;
The blinds hang crazy and the shingles blow away,
The fields have gone back to broomsedge and pine,
And the soil washes down the red gulley scars.
With so much to be done, there's no time for being bitter.
Your father made it for us, it is up to you to save it,
What is past is over, and you should not be bitter."
But my brother is bitter, and he does not hear.

Memo: For the Race Orators

I

This nigger too should be in history,
This black man amply deserves his fame:
    The traitor, the spy, the coward, the renegade,
    The currier of favors, the lickspittle fawner for privilege,
    The beaten who lived in dread of the singing whip,
    The Judas who sold his brother for a price,
    Looking for power, looking for gratitude,
    An easier place, or just not to be beaten.

II

Enroll these historic events and persons:
    When Gabriel led his thousand on Richmond,
    Armed with clubs and scythe-swords fashioned in spare time,
    Down on the well-stocked powder-house and arsenal,
    Remember Tom and Pharaoh, who blurted the news
    To Mister Mosby, and sought as reward
    What Gabriel wanted to fight and die for.

    Record the waiting men "grateful for presents of old coats,"
    Colonel Prioleau's cook and house-boy, Devany,
    Contented, preparing viands fit for a master,
    Happy, when house guests torpidly beamed.
    Tell of his serving the news up hot:
    Vesey is plotting, the Negroes are gathering,
    We must do something, the slaves are crazy,
    The house guests and fine houses and gardens are threatened.

And Jim the driver, who peeked in the window,
When Cuffee wrapped the hoe-cake and hunk of side-meat
And a twist of tobacco in the bandanna,
And stole out of doors on the moonless night.
The grapevine had told Cuffee: way down in Florida
On the Appalachicola, with the Seminoles and Spaniards
You will be free, Cuffee, you will be free.
Tell of Jim's flight, swifter even than Cuffee's,

Of the dogs treeing Cuffee in less than an hour
Sick at heart, still on his master's land.

Tell of Sandy, worth a thousand dollars as a slave
On the auction block, worth much less as a man.
Wavering, drawn to the fire of the young Fred Douglass,
Torn between the preacher's "Servants obey your masters."
And Douglass' hissed speech: "A man must be free."
At night times dreaming of a bird of prey
With Douglass in his talons, flying southwest,
Seeing it as plain as he ever saw Douglass.
When they locked up the plotters, Sandy was freed,
His eyes shifted and dropped when Douglass looked at him.

And the hackman who raised the hue and cry
When the seventy-odd fugitives sailed down the Potomac
And Stonestreet, the informer, who got in the graces
Of the runaways lurking in waterfront holes,
Overtrustful in Washington, stronghold of liberty,
And sold them back across the Potomac
And drank well on the thirty pieces of silver.

And the faint of heart, following Harriet Tubman,
Jeopardizing the safety of all
To still his own fears of the dogs and the silence
And the zigzag thrust into the unknown,
Superstitiously dreading the small dark woman
So much like a man, so fierce, so grim,
Who would not talk, who would not explain,
Who would not grow tired, who drove them on
More merciless than any overseer of a gang.
He blubbered: "I wants to go back. I wants
To get home. . . . I don't want no freedom. I wants—"
Quailed before the eye that he thought was evil,
Before the slow words, no louder than a whisper,
Before the big pistol she whipped from her dress:
"A dead nigger tells no tales. Nigger, go on or die."

III

Let this man have his innings in your oratory.

Show how he remains: a runner to the master,
To the time-keeper, the warden, the straw-boss, the brass-hat,
The top-hat, the big shot, the huge noise, the power,
Show him running, hat in his hand,
Yelping, his tail and his hindquarters drooping.

Listen, orator, high-collared, full-bosom shirted,
With your full-dress version of race achievement
Of heroes who worked up to full dress too
Put this man where he belongs.

In your corridor of history,
Put this rat in the hold
Of your ship of progress,
This dry-rot in the rungs
Of your success ladder,
This rampant blot
On your race escutcheon,
This bastard in the line
Of race genealogy.

Celebrate this nigger.
He has enough descendants
To hear about their illustrious sire.

Crossing

This is not Jordan River
There lies not Canaan
There is still
One more wide river to cross.

This is the Mississippi
And the stars tell us only
That this is not the road.

We do not know
If any have reached that Canaan
We have received no word.

Behind us the belling pack
Beyond them the hunters
Before us the dismal swamp.

We do not know. . . .

We have exchanged Louisiana for Mississippi
Merely
Georgia for Florida
Carolina for Tennessee.

We have passed, repassed
So many rivers
Okmulgee, Chattahoochee,
St. Mary's, Mississippi,
Alabama, Tennessee,
Mississippi.

We have leapt
From swamp land
Into marshes
We have won through
To bloodred clay
To gravel and rock
To the baked lands
To the scorched barrens.

And we grow footsore
And muscle weary
Our faces grow sullen
And our hearts numb

We do not know. . . .

We know only
That there lies not Canaan
That this is no River Jordan.

Still are we motherless children
Still are we dragging travelers
Alone, and a long ways from home.

Still with the hard earth for our folding bed
Still with our head pillowed upon a rock

And still
With one more river,
Oh, one wide river to cross.

Call for Barnum

Conversation in the smoker:
We oughta hav a Barnum. We put on these shows,
Good shows, too, what these folks can understand,
And a measly five thousand is all that turns out.
Lemme give you the set-up. They knew about this nigger
Knew he was a halfwit: he grabbed hisself a wench.
Only last year, but we let the bastard go—
Took mercy on him—he carried a row all right
A right smart worker, and the girl was black besides.

Wal, everybody coulda told you we was gonna get him
He was one of these guys just had to grab at women
And so, with the crops laid by, and the boys all primed
Word was sent around as to when the show would start
The radio announced it; a buddy of mine came
All the way from Baltimore to see the good time.
He said to me he always liked a circus in the country.

And still we ain't had but a frazzling four thousand.
Why think of a crowd at a world series game.
And I swear it was a good show we put on.
All the folks there and plenty excitement
Road cops standing by, making their bluff,
Say, some of the dumb birds tried carrying it out,
But a coupla split skulls persuaded 'em different.

As good as a movie. In the nick of time
Soon as the sheriff and the big-shots fixed alibis
The old gang charged. I was up with the leaders.

We beat in the jaildoor, went up and got the bastard,
Took him for a little stroll, then let him have it.
All a crowd could want. Steel, hemp, lead, gasoline.
Plenty for your money, with some drinks thrown in,
And a scramble for souvenirs, to a pretty chorus
"Give us all something to remember you by."

The only fault I can see was that the damned rope broke
Got him away when we only had one ear
Some folks, I'd say, take their badges too serious.

But we split up the rope, and we got his gold teeth.
The rest wa'nt no real loss, all burnt anyhow.

And, I'm tellin' you there were only four thousand.

For a show like that. It beats me, I swear.

But there'll be another show soon, maybe better.
I'll let you know, ahead, the place and the hour.
We'll make up a party, the madames and all.
Nothing to be scared of; the wrong guns don't go off
And we kick the tear-gas cans around like footballs.
I know you'll like it. It'll be right educational.
And bring the kiddies along. They'll shore have fun.

Song of Triumph

Let the band play Dixie.
And let the Rebel Yell resound.
Let daughters of the Confederacy
Be proud that once more virginal loveliness
Even in dingy courtrooms
Receives the homage of the poets.

Let us rush to Stone Mountain
Uncover our heads, stand speechless before
Granite embodiments of our knighthood
Unfinished but everlasting,
"And truth and honor established here, forever."
Lo! Stonewall, preux chevalier,
And Lee, majestic Arthur, facing East.

Behind them, to the West
Scottsboro, Decatur.
Eight cowering Negroes in a jail
Waiting for the justice
Chivalry as ever extends to them,
Still receiving the benefactions
Of *Noblesse Oblige.*

Oh, let us be proud.
Oh, let us, undefeated, raise again
The Rebel Yell.

Remembering Nat Turner

(For R. C. L.)

We saw a bloody sunset over Courtland, once Jerusalem,
As we followed the trail that old Nat took
When he came out of Cross Keys down upon Jerusalem,
In his angry stab for freedom a hundred years ago.
The land was quiet, and the mist was rising,
Out of the woods and the Nottaway swamp,
Over Southampton the still night fell,
As we rode down to Cross Keys where the march began.

When we got to Cross Keys, they could tell us little of him,
The Negroes had only the faintest recollections:
    "I ain't been here so long, I come from up roun' Newsome;
    Yassah, a town a few miles up de road,
    The old folks who coulda told you is all dead an' gone.
    I heard something, sometime; I doan jis remember what.
    'Pears lak I heard that name somewheres or other.
    So he fought to be free. Well. You doan say."

An old white woman recalled exactly
How Nat crept down the steps, axe in his hand,
After murdering a woman and child in bed,
"Right in this here house at the head of these stairs"
(In a house built long after Nat was dead).
She pointed to a brick store where Nat was captured,
(Nat was taken in the swamp, three miles away)
With his men around him, shooting from the windows
(She was thinking of Harpers Ferry and old John Brown).
She cackled as she told how they riddled Nat with bullets
(Nat was tried and hanged at Courtland, ten miles away).
She wanted to know why folks would comes miles
Just to ask about an old nigger fool.
    "Ain't no slavery no more, things is going all right,
    Pervided thar's a good goober market this year.
    We had a sign post here with printing on it,
    But it rotted in the hole, and thar it lays,
    And the nigger tenants split the marker for kindling.
    Things is all right, now, ain't no trouble with the niggers
    Why they make this big to-do over Nat?"

As we drove from Cross Keys back to Courtland,
Along the way that Nat came down upon Jerusalem,
A watery moon was high in the cloud-filled heavens,
The same moon he dreaded a hundred years ago.
The tree they hanged Nat on is long gone to ashes,
The trees he dodged behind have rotted in the swamps.

The bus for Miami and the trucks boomed by,
And touring cars, their heavy tires snarling on the pavement.
Frogs piped in the marshes, and a hound bayed long,
And yellow lights glowed from the cabin windows.

As we came back the way that Nat led his army,
Down from Cross Keys, down to Jerusalem,
We wondered if his troubled spirit still roamed the Nottaway,
Or if it fled with the cock-crow at daylight,
Or lay at peace with the bones in Jerusalem,
Its restlessness stifled by Southampton clay.

We remembered the poster rotted through and falling,
The marker split for kindling a kitchen fire.

Part Five
ROAD TO THE LEFT

Raise a Song

Remember:
      How on the reeking schooner,
      Ushered on deck, for exercise, the stranger tribesmen,
      Their grass huts far behind, over the widening waters,
      Were coaxed, starved into song;
      Their legs and feet whipped into dancing
      Into ghastly imitations of joy. . . .

      And in the rice marshes, and the cotton rows,
      Or cutting and grinding cane, or on the levee wharves
      How they sang, commanded by overseers and drivers:
          Juba, Juba

Gonna raise a ruckus tonight
Mas'r bought a yaller gal
He bought her from the south
Look away, look away:
Coonjine!

And how, on Mr. Harriman's line,
Mr. Jaygoozi's, Mr. Jim Hill's,
The Polacks with their guitars
The Dagoes with their accordians,
The Hunkies with their fiddles
The Dutchies with their zithers
The niggers with their banjoes
Forgot the bitterness of the driving days
Raising their songs
So the steel roads girded the prairies.

And how, in the tabernacles
Before the rancid soup, the lusty song must be raised
Jesus' blood can make me whole
Before the knotty mattress of the flophouse
Could creak beneath the wobbly's aching bones
    There is a happy land,
    Far, far away

And how the Y.M.C.A. boys over the hot chocolate
Tried to whip up a musical sweat
With "Good morning, Mr. Zip, Zip, Zip,
    With your hair cut just as short as mine"
Wheedled ferocity with "Keep your head down, Fritzy boy"
Paid off religious dues: "Onward Christian soldiers"
(But the boys slogging through the mudholes,
tumbling in bravado to their deaths,
With a song on their lips, or in despair
Drunkenness or sick fear at their triphammer hearts
The brave, the brave, flung smack in the teeth of death,
Planked square between the eyes of death
A ribald chorus:
Mademoiselle from Armentieres
Parley-vous
Hinky, dinky, parley-vous.)

Remember. . . .

Oh makers of America, oh meeters in board rooms
So that the mines will stay open, the sweat shops awake,
The factory wheels be whirring, the cranes traveling,
The harvests be threshed and the freight cars loaded,

Teach the evicted veteran
His paltry few sticks and boards on the sidewalk
Their disrepair shameful to him
Teach him to carry the lead
Of "Home, Sweet Home"

Teach the breadlines, waiting for the gruel,
Stamping their paper thin soles
Against the biting coldness of the concrete
To sing four part chorus to America, The Beautiful

O makers of America, so that America be made
Give to us bread and circuses,
And raise us a song!

Colloquy

(BLACK WORKER AND WHITE WORKER)

"It's been a long time since we got together, Sam."
"A long time? I don't know when we did befo'."
"Sure you remember when we was kids,
Long time ago?"

"I recollec' how you chased me and my brothers
Out of de crick; an' I recollec' when
You rocked us through Cottontown clean cross de railroad—
We didn't get together, then.

"We didn't get together 'cause we niggers ran too fast.
We knew we'd keep our health a little better if we run,
That's about all de gettin' together
You an' me's ever done."

"Reckon you'se right—we 'uns been tarnation onery,
But we didn't know no better, an' that time's past.
I got to stop my pitchin' rocks, an' you—you got to trust me,
An' not run away so fas'.

"The bosses got us both where de bosses want us
An' dey's squeezin' us both an' dey won't let go.
We gotta get together, we gotta jerk from under
Or else we are goners, bo."

"I coulda told you, long ago, Mist' Charlie,
Bein' onery wan't no way you should behave,
When both of us got more'n our share of misery
From rockin' cradle to de lastin' grave."

"Shake hands, Sam. We'll be buddies now.
An' do our scrappin' side by side from this."
"Well, here's my hand. I never gave it before,
Scared I might draw back a wrist.

"But dere's hard times comin'—wuss'n hard times now.
An' in de hard times dat I recollec'

De whites stood together on top of our shoulders
An' give it to us square in de neck.

"So I tells you like de bull frog say unto de eagle,
Flyin' cross de stone quarry high in de sky,
Don't do it, big boy, don't do it to me—
Not when we'se up so high. . . ."

Street Car Gang

For the bread for the children,
The cheap shoes, the overcoat,
For the rent, for the number runner,
The insurance dues,
The shot of gin, the earrings for the broad
The Saturday dance
The new strings on the guitar:
     The drill splattering the asphalt
     The shovelfuls of rock
     The picks, the creaking of wheelbarrows

      For the finishing academy
      The golf courses, the jodhpurs
      The country club soirees,
      The clipped coupons
From the drill, the picks, the shovels,
The trembling jerks in the arms,
The shattering, persistent, in the nerves,
The metallic tattoo upon the eardrums
   Man, las' night it was jes' too much
   Man, I couldn't get no sleep at all;

          For the trip to Europe
The cold gray daybreak
The soggy lunch
Salt sweats in the mouth
Dried sweat upon the faded shirt
       For the divorce fees
       For the kept lady's apartment

The aching bones, the embittered heart
   For the bread for the children
The self abasement, when the dressed up frails and dudes
Shrink in the crowded car
The bravado of the loud guffaw
Of the switchblade reasserting manhood
Of the canned heat for forgetting

    For the food for the kids
    The perfume for the broad
    The dime for the pastor

But from the drill, as well,
From the pick, the shovel:
The banded arms; the corded shoulders,
The will, trained to doggedness
  He's a young'un,
  But he can take it
The hope, sucking strength from bitterness
  Caint stay this way forever:
And a strengthening mind
Taking stock of the weaklings
On top now by luck or craft
  There's something here going on wrong
  By Gawd we do the work
  By Gawd we earn the pay
And someday the will and the mind
Drilling through concrete:
  By Gawd we do the work
  What come from it is ours
  We got us one more job:
  This thing been messed up too long
  Time to get these rails laid straight.

  We better get it
  Fixed up
  Right.

Side by Side

Listen, John Cracker; hear me, Joe Nigg.
You on one side of the railroad, you on the other.
This railroad track is no final separation.
This eighteen foot cut isn't a canyon.

Your shanty is shaky, John, the roof is leaky,
The same wind whistles through yours and Joe's.

And grits, and molasses like grease for belts,
And chicory coffee and collards like jimson
Are the same on both sides of the track.
And the side meat comes from the same place on the hog.

And sweat and filth
Are not so different
Even on the preferred side of the track.

Bridges can be stretched, have been stretched across railroads
Especially over one horse lines like this.

II. THE TRAIN

Take the train, John; get on board, Joe.

Where do you ride it, where does it take you?
A few miles down the road to a funeral.
"I been down to Gainesville to bury my mother."
It takes you a few miles up to a marriage.
"But how thay gonna make out? Jim ain't got no job."
It rolls you to a frolic, a protracted meeting,
A corn-drinking spree, a hot old time in the town,
It carries you both, safely handcuffed, to jail.

Listen, John, does Joe's riding up front in the Jimmy
Sweeten so much the dull grits of your days?

When you get where you're going, are you not still
John the po' cracker, Joe the po' nig?

Is it so much to rare back for a hot minute's riding
First class, while Joe rares back in his half-a-car.
Save up a week's wages, plank it down for a ticket
Shut your way back to the Pullman and diners.
The classy folks propped up back there
Want the conductor to move you back to your coach.

III. SCRATCHED

I heard a pool-room philosopher cracking:
    "Po' whites is the cue-ball, niggers the eight-ball,
      Cue-ball knocked the eight-ball sprang in the pocket
      Then scratch itself; so eightball and cueball
      Both in the pocket, and the game is done."

IV. HALLELUJAH HALLELU

Your unpainted, ramshackly churches stand
Side by side, Lord, side by side.

In one John hears of hell for sinners,
Of heaven for the hard-worked, meek, long-suffering;
In the other Joe hears of heaven bright heaven,
For the meek, long-suffering, hard-worked,
And of hell for sinners.

John Cracker knows that hell gapes wide for Joe.
Joe Nigg believes hell is hungry for John.

John's hardshelled religious is a little harder,
Lacquered over with Calvin and John Knox;

Joe's hard-shell is a bit thinner and lined
With a few strange tracings from Africa.

And both of you shout and both of you writhe
And your preachers black and white pound on the Bible,

Stamp on the pulpit, preach a seventh day hell,
Make you forget the hell of six days.

V. FACTORY

John in his blue denim, and faded gray shirt,
Joe in his gray faded shirt and blue denim,
I have seen you burst forth from the factory
When the Abe Lincoln noon-whistle blasted you free,
For one hot hour; I have seen you peering
Into lunch-pails, hoping for surprise.
John on this lading platform, Joe on the other,
Separate still.

But the hour was only sixty minutes for John,
The bucket of lunch still poor fuel for burning
In the pay envelope that John draws there is little
More than Joe's pittance, but it serves, it serves
Not John, but the men in tall office building

Sipping their highballs beneath turning fans,
The men at the golf-course, at the country-clubs,
The men in the buffet cars, diners and Pullmans.

Let the white workers strike, will break it with niggers
Then let the niggers if they dare.

They know how to keep you separate, separate,
Poor white trash and nigger trash, side by side.

VI. THE WOMEN-FOLK

John Cracker, your daughters, barefoot through the day,
Put on silk stockings and shoes and gay print dresses,
Go down to the station to see the evening mail go through.
They stand on the cinders and wave to the engineer.

Joe Nigg, your daughters, barefoot through the day,
Put on silk stocking and shoes and gay print dresses,

Go down to the station to see the evening mail go through.
From the stack of crossties they wave to the Pullman porters and waiters.

Both are hungry for more than the men they know,
Standing on cinders, or sitting on crossties;
Side by side.

Your wives, Mrs. John Cracker and Aunt Josey Nigg,
Two women forgotten on a Georgia clay slope,
Sometimes cross the railroad divide
Ignore the whistle that blows far away,
The smudge of smoke down the line,
Forget sometimes and talk.

Aunt Josey knows what to do for sick children,
Mrs. John has a new way to fix up greens.

Mrs. John's first son is making time on the roads of the county,
Aunt Josey's boy is picking cotton on a convict farm.
They may meet yet in Fulton Tower,
Side by side, Lord, side by side.

VII. MOB

A nigger killed a white man in the neighborhood
The nigger was shot up and then hung out
For the blood to dry, a black sponge dripping red.
John, you were in the mob, and what did it get you?

The killed man is just as dead as the lynched,
And both busted hell wide, wide open,
And side by side, Lord, side by side.

VIII. MUSIC

You on your side, on your harmonica,
Mix mournful blues with hill-billy tunes;
Joe sings Barbara Allen with some Tom-Tom swing.

John sings of a knight coming riding, riding
With rings and gold and gear;
Joe sings to a guitar of a sweet chariot
Swinging low for to carry him home.

Listen, John:
The son you looked for to ransom you,
To pay up the rent, to fill the cupboard,
He did not come home, riding in triumph,
The train brought the poor linthead home to die.

Listen Joe:
That sweet chariot is running late

Either they've taken it off the line,
Or routed it somewheres else.

Listen, John:
But you will probably never listen,
Your ears have been deafened by the roar so long,
You have told yourself there is nothing Joe can say
But "Yessuh" and "Nawsuh," and "Be right there, Mister John"

You have never got around to it, John,
Either to listening or thinking.

But Joe has said it, in moments when fear
Did not catch his tongue and throttle his breath:
    "Mr. John, Mr. John
    We cain't never make it dis way at all."

Listen, John Cracker,
Joe Nigg, I've an earful for yo.

Part Six
FRILOT COVE

Let Us Suppose

Let us suppose him differently placed,
In wider fields than these bounded by bayous
And the fringes of moss-hung trees
Over which, in lazy spirals, the caranchos soar and dip.

Let us suppose these horizons pushed farther,
So that his eager mind,
His restless senses, his swift eyes,
Could glean more than the sheaves he stored
Time and time again:
Let us suppose him far away from here.

Or let us, keeping him here, suppose him
More submissive, less ready for the torrents of hot Cajun speech,
The clenched fist, the flushed face,
The proud scorn and the spurting anger,
The proper slant to his neck, the eyes abashed,
Let us suppose his tender respect for his honor
Calloused; his debt to himself outlawed.
Let us suppose him what he could never be.
Let us suppose him less thrifty,
Less the hustler from early morning until first dark,
Let us suppose his corn weedy,
His cotton rusty, scantily fruited, and his fat mules poor,
His cane a sickly yellow
Like his white neighbor's.

Let us suppose his burnt brick color,
His shining hair thrown back from his forehead,
His stalwart shoulders, his lean hips,
His gently fused patois of Cajun, Indian, African,
Let us suppose these less urgent
To her, who might have been less lonesome,
Less driven by Louisiana heat, by lone flat days.
And less hungry.

Let us suppose his full-throated laugh
Less repulsive to the crabbed husband,
Let us suppose his swinging strides
Less of an insult to the half-alive scarecrow
Of the neighboring fields:
Let us suppose him less fermenting to hate.

Let us suppose that there had been
In this tiny forgotten parish, among these lost bayous,
No imperative need
Of preserving unsullied, Anglo-Saxon mastery.

Let us suppose—
Oh, let us suppose him alive.

Cloteel

Cloteel:
Rampart Street knows you now: the golden
           decked saloons
The curtained off rooms, behind the latticed
           windows
The late morning sun creeps through
In warm bars upon your half-stirring,
           cream-skinned body
Your eyes have grown bold and direct and
           your twisted mouth
Is quick with pitiless speech.
Only now and again, across the jangling
The loud strut cries, the jets of laughter,
High pitched quarreling, the drunken yells
The klaxons and the sirens, the grinding of
           trucks
The clatter of rickety wagons,
Over and beyond the whistles blasting
           noon

A church bell sounds, and then your arrogant head
Bows low
And you go back, skipping the long, long months

You hear
Distantly tolling the dull Angelus
Over the sleepy town as you last heard it,
May gone, Mother's Day, two years ago, now.

They think of you often there
As a lil biddy, your large eyes shy and frightened
Among the crêpe myrtles, and the thick, thick vines
Colorful as the princess plumes, sweet as
           magnolia blossoms,
Your swift bare feet padding down the
           gray lanes
Or older,
Leading the cotton row, your happiness 'sahcy,'
Your jokes filling the wagon rattling home;

Or eager in the dance, your olive face a flush,
Your mouth two petals, and your wide, soft eyes
Seeking, unanswered;
Or talking to the priest, strict Catholic then,
Your mind a query, your restless body awake . . .
O *ma chère*
Rampart Street knows you now, the screened
                in balconies
The furtive dark streets, and the long,
                shuttered doors.

The shrill piping whistles, the noonday blast
From New Orleans factories, the crazy wails
From the levees, the blues of the sidewalk shops,
The static of the blaring radios for you are hushed,
And you decline your head, and your slim fingers grope.

Faintly but clearly now, old church bells peal
The Angels' bells ring out over the sleepy town.

Yes, they remember you there. . . .

Parish Doctor

They come to him for subscriptions
They resent examination, investigation
They tell *him* what is wrong with them,
       They *know.*

It is pus on de heart, hole in de head
The maul is open, they got stummatache,
Somebody let some night air in the battens.
They want him only to subscribe,
The *medcins:* bitter-bitter is the best.

"Docteur, I doan b'leeve you can do nottin
           fuh me

I got a snake in me. I know, me, I been
           spelled.

You laugh, mon? I tell you son, a snake he in
           my inside."

He tells them he's the best conjuh doctor, best
           for roots and herbs,

North of New Orleans. They pop their eyes;

"You tink he know dose ting for true?"

They drink the boiled juices of a jit black hen
For diarrhea, for consumption
They kill a jit black dog, bury him three days,
           then cook him

And oil the ailing person with the grease;
For rheumatism they kill a turkey buzzard,
Dry him up; rub the stiff jints with the mess.
But jit black dogs and *caranchos* are none
           too plentiful.
They come to see their docteur, when these fail.

They like him; young, good-looking, easy laugher,
As brown as they and one of theirs forever.
The women call him *cher:* tender but embarrassed.
Their good men pass sly glances at his
                    clipped moustache.

They think he lies about the conjuh knowledge
But still he got sharp eyes, you never know.
They pay him off with garden truck and cane
                    juice.

One auntie brought him six hens tied together
Squawking and screaming enough to wake a
                    graveyard.

One hen was jit-black to help him fix his
                    medcins.

One night, past midnight, we jolted twelve miles to
                    a cabin

It seemed as if the Ford would never make it.
"Tank Gawd, you'se here. I tole'em you would
                    get here.

He's hurted bad. He caught a bullet in his laig.
Tank Gawd, you'se come." In the dull light of
                    the lamp.

I watched his skillful probing for the slug.
Outside the ring of light, dark faces watched us,
His fingers were deft and gentle. The woman's
                    sobbing

Quieted; the man on the table lay there
                    sweating

Breathing heavily, but trusting; his eyes rolled
Following the hands.

Uncle Joe

Unc' Joe, *c'est drôle.*

"Hot dawg it, but it's hot-hot dis mawnin.
I wouldn't pick a pon' uh cotton today.
Not fuh all de money in de Opelousas Bank.
How you feel, yosef, son?
Lemme try some uh yo' store bought tobacco.
Umph. Cocktail tobacco."
He filled his corncob and, grinning,
Dropped the generous leavings in his shirt pocket.

He worked away on his letter beneath the fig-tree.
"Son," he called. "Is they uh a in eight?
No? I thought it didn't add up right.
I always wanted to go to one uh dem
Universaries and other high schools.
Yo sho' dat you a teacher?
You doan ack much like a teacher to me.
You ain't got, nohow, de teacher's talk.
Mos' times, I can make out tings wat *you* say.
My boy he went to school, my gal she graduate.
We got de picture in the parlor. Sho. I read printing but not writing;
I can speak Créole and Américain.
Bon Dieu me péni. How you make dat out?
See, you don't know. Me, I knows good.
I talk Américain so you kin make me out.
I 'member when ole man Thibodeaux he say,
Old Thibodeaux, he brother to sheriff uh dis parish,
He beg me, 'Joe, don't send yo' chillen to school.
Don't luh 'em to read.' He so sad he mos' cry.
But me? I pay Thibodeaux no mind at all, at all.

"Me, I doan pay nobody no mind. Not too much mind.
I 'member when de sheriff and dem others,
Git hot after de boy from de penitentiary
I see de game-leg boy when he bust in de thicket.
Ole sheriff Thibodeaux and de others ride up,
De moonlight jes a glittin' on dey long gun bar'ls.
Dey axe me 'Where he?' and I say 'Who he?'
An' Didee Lebon he say luh him

Rawhide it outa old Unc' Joe. And Unc' Joe
He jes' look at Didee and he say to de sheriff,
'You have two men to hunt on dis trip if Didee
Lay a rawhide on me, or a finger, too.' And dey depart on dey horses.
And soon I hear de guns go 'Clap-Boom, Clap-Boom!'
Great Gawd amighty, but that was shootin'!
An' when I went to de Cath'lic Church at Villeplatte
Wid my mother, she daid now, the good God forgive me
Do red-bones—who dey? De Cajans is red-bones,
We call 'em crawfish eaters, powder pans, red-bones
Mean enough to be called anyting you got mind to.
So one Sunday on de way home dey surround us
In our buggy, and throw up dey big hats
To scare our mule, but our mule don't scare good.
And at Papa Lastrape's gate dey put up a rail.
And gimme de dare to take it down.
Dey had dey shotguns across dey saddles,
But dey had to have some good reason to mob us up,
Cause dey hadn't so long left Father Antoine.
Well, I ain't scared, an' my ma she don't scare.
I didn't say nottin'. She didn't say nottin'!
But I had heart enough to take de rail down.
So dey talked aroun', den dey galloped off whoopin'
Into de woods, an' a shootin' dey guns.
Den, dey luh us alone. But me I'm Baptist now."

He looked at me, and grinned, and then I grinned.
"You know, I gret big liar, me," he said.
"But still I kin do what I gots to do.
And dats no lie." And me, I knew it wasn't.

Unc' Joe, c'est drôle.
Uncle Joe is all right by me.

Louisiana Pastoral

"I gots to be gon now; we ding potaht."

I remember her in her too large overalls
Her sweet brown face shadow-darkened by the huge blue bonnet

She clambered in the wagon with the sacks and ploughs.
Her husband waved me "howdo" and "Aur'voir."

Her house was full of *jolies petis filles*
In her yard the crepe myrtles were in flower.

Over the lush green fields, past the strutting ram
And his inquisitive awe, over the drying black mud gulley
The wagon bumped and rattled; once, nearly thrown, she grabbed
Her husband's arm, a soft laugh floated back.

Oh little child mother; oh peti belle Creole
May your *bon Dieu* keep you your happiness. . . .

Part Seven
WASHINGTON, D.C.

Glory, Glory

When Annie Mae Johnson condescends to take the air,
Give up all your business, make haste to get there,
Glory oh glory, get there, be there.

The last time I saw Annie on the avenue,
She held up traffic for an hour or two.
The green light refused, absolutely, to go off at all;
And the red light and the amber nearly popped the glass,
When Annie walked by, they came on so fast,
Then stayed on together twenty minutes after she went past;
And it took three days for to get them duly timed again.
Even so, they palpitated every now and then.

A driver of a coal truck turned his head around,
Watching her walk and knocked an old man down,
Old man's weak eyes had been dazzled by the gorgeous sight;
Po' man collapsed and he heaved a sigh,
Said, "Lord, I'm willin' at the last to die,
Cause my state is blessed, everything's all right,
Happy, Lord, happy, yes happy am I."

Saw a Rock Creek Bridge car jump off the track,
Do the shim-sham shimmy and come reeling back;
Saw a big steam roller knocked clean off its base,
When it got itself together, the little Austin had its place.

Ambulance came a-clanging, the fire truck banging,
Police patrol a-sailing, the sirens all wailing,
Parked any whichaway and turned their headlights high,
With their engines just a purring, till Annie Mae tipped on by.

Folks gathered from the manors, swarmed in from the alleys,
Deserted their pool-rooms, rushed out of their lodges,
Some took taxis to get them to the place on time;
Way the preachers left their congregations was a holy crime.
Twixt Uncle Ham's sonny boys and Aunt Hagar's daughters
Just like Daddy Moses through the Red Sea Waters,
Annie Johnson made a path, as she laid it on the frazzling line;
The dark waves parted, and then they closed in behind.

Aaanh, Lord, when Annie Mae lays it down,
If you want to take the census proper, better come around.

Choices

Don't want no yaller gal, dat's a color will not stay,
Don't want no yaller, yaller nevah known to stay,
Git caught in a storm, de yaller sho' will fade away.

Don't want no pretty pink, pink ain't de shade fo' me,
Don't want no pretty pink, pink it ain't de shade fo' me.
When you think you's got her, ain't nuffin' but yo' used to be.

Don't want no black gal, gums blue lak de sea,
Don't want no blue gums, blue jus' lak de deep blue sea,
Fraid that when I kiss her, bluine run all over me.

Don't want no brownskin, choklit to de bone,
Don't want no brownskin, choklit to de bone,
Choklit melts jes lak vanilla, and runs all out de cone.

Don't want no charcoal, soot's a mess what I despise,
Don't want no charcoal, soot's a mess what I despise,
Want to know whah my gal's at, anytime she shets her eyes.

Don't want no Geechie gal, talkin' lak a nachel zoo,
Don't want no Geechie, talkin' lak a nachel zoo,
Jabber lak a monkey, make a monkey outa you.

Don't care for de Ofays, got no dealins wif Miss Ann,
Don't care for de Ofay, got no dealins wif Miss Ann,
Don't lak her brother Hemp, nor her cousin Mr. Cool Oil Can.

Don't want me no Injin, no Injin squaw of red,
Don't want me no Injin, no Injin squaw of red,
Ain't got much hair, want it left on top my frazzly head.

Don't want no blue woman, moanin' wid de lonesome blues,
Don't want no blue woman, moanin' wid de graveyard blues,
Got mo' blues myself now dan a man could evah use.

Gonna git me a green gal, if a green gal's to be found,
Git me a green gal, if a green gal is to be found,
But I spec' she ain't born yet, and her mama she in the ground.

No More Worlds to Conquer

My boy Alec is a smart bootlegger
He's a race man now and not anybody's Nigger,
And the cars he rides in get bigger and bigger.

He started with a Kettle, and he peddled in a Ford
But now he is reaping his well earned reward,
With a Packard for himself and a Hudson for his broad.

He moves from the slums to the dickty section
And his shrewd advance in the right direction
Makes chances slim for Alexander's detection.

And now he has for customers Senators and such,
He admits his early comrades don't amount to much,
So now he barely speaks to his old boy Dutch.

He forgets the cooncan, and Georgia skin he played,
For the sake of contract contacts he has made,
And his stomps become 'bals' in the Colonade.

He sees a poor drunk on Florida Avenue
And is pierced by nausea through and through
And he wonders what the race is coming to.

   MORAL

If we only had the brains that are his,
We too could be great like my boy is
Magnates in the world's great businesses!

Call Boy

Git out o' bed, you rascals,
Take it up from de covers,
Bring it to de strawboss
Fast as you can;
Down to de railroads
De day is beginnin',
An' day never waited
Fo' no kinda man.

Sun's jes a-peekin'
Over top o' de mountains,
An' de fogclouds a-liftin'
Fo' de break of day;
Number Forty-four's pantin',
Takin' on coal an' water,
An' she's strainin' ready
Fo' to git away.

Leave yo' wives an' yo' sweethearts,
Yo' pink and yo' yaller,
Yo' blue black and stovepipe,
Yo' chocolate brown;
All you backbitin' rascals,
Leave de other men's women,
De night crew from de roundhouse
Is a-roundin' roun'.

O you shifters and humpers,
You boiler washers,
You oilers and you greasers
Of de drivin' rods,
You switchers and flagmen,
Tile layers and tampers,
Youse wanted at de Norfolk
And Western yards.

You cooks got to cook it
From here to Norfolk,
You waiters got to dish it
From here to Tennessee,

You porters got to run
From here to Memphis,
Gotta bring de man's time,
Dontcha see, dontcha see?

De air may be cold, an'
Yo' bed may be easy,
Yo' babe may be comfy
An' warm by yo' side;
But don't snore so loud
Dat you can't hear me callin',
Don't ride no nightmare,
Dere's engines to ride.

Git up off o' yo shirt-tails,
You dumb lazy rounders,
Think I'm gonna let you
Sleep all day?
Bed has done ruint
Dem as can't leave it,
You knows you can't make it
Actin' datway. . . .

Puttin' on Dog

Look at old Scrappy puttin' on dog,
Puttin' on dog, puttin' on dog,
Look at old Scrappy puttin' on dog,
Steppin' like nobody's business.

With a brandnew silk shirt pink as a sunset,
With a pair of suspenders blue as the sky,
With bulldog brogans red as a clay road—
Pull up, mule wagons, let the mail train by.

Look at old Scrappy puttin' on dog,
Puttin' on dog, puttin' on dog,
Look at old Scrappy puttin' on dog,
Todle-oh-in' with his Jane.

Rared back at the wheel with his arm around his baby,
Heads his old flivver out of the town,
And Buck's mad enough to chew a fistful of staples,
And drink Sloan's liniment to wash 'em down.

Look at old Scrappy puttin' on dog,
Puttin' on dog, puttin' on dog,
Look at old Scrappy puttin' on dog,
Down in Pap Silas' poolroom.

He's about to use English on the lonesome eight ball
Stops short when he hears what Buck has said,
Winds up like Babe Ruth aimin' for a homer
And bends his cuestick around Buck's head.

Look at old Scrappy puttin' on dog,
Puttin' on dog, puttin' on dog,
Look at old Scrappy puttin' on dog,
Bustin' rock on the county road.

He laughed with his lawyers, and he winked at the judge,
Stuck his fingers up his nose at the jury in the dock,
Waved good-by to the gals when they sent him to the workgang,
And even had his own way of bustin' up rock.

Look at old Scrappy puttin' on dog,
Puttin' on dog, puttin' on dog,
Look at old Scrappy puttin' on dog,
Callin' for the bad man Buck.

Buck saw him comin', pulled his thirty-two forty,
Got him once in the arm, and twice in the side;
Scrappy switched his gat, like they do it in the Western,
And let the daylight into Buck's black hide.

Look at old Scrappy puttin' on dog,
Puttin' on dog, puttin' on dog,
Look at old Scrappy puttin' on dog,
Waitin' for the undertaker's wagon.

In his box-back coat and his mutt-leg britches,
And a collar high enough for to choke a ox;
And the girls stopped cryin' when they saw how Scrappy
Was a-puttin' on dog in a pinewood box.

O you rascal, puttin' on dog,
Puttin' on dog, puttin' on dog,
O you rascal, puttin' on dog,
Great Gawd, but you was a man!

Part Eight
REMEMBRANCES

April in Coolwell

I know that I shall never see the rain
Sift like a mist through snowbloomed apple trees,
Shall never hear this fluting song again
Without remembering swift joys like these.
Two happy children in this dreamy weather,
Gypsy and impudent, loved hotly here,
Forecasting sure that soon, no more together
We straggle through less lucky seasons, dear.

Whatever then my weariness, despair,
Will be laid by; oh always then for me
A trim ghost running lightly here and there

On wet turf strewn with petals; carefree laughter
Will blend with wind and rain forever after,
And I shall well recall our Arcady. . . .

Coolwell Vignette

(FROM VIRGINIA WOODS)

There is not much that he would ask for now.
The axe whirls in the air, pauses, descends,
Is buried deep in hardened locust fiber.
The slender handle quivers for a while
And then subsides. A broadened boyish smile
Lights up a face already glistening
From mist of sweat spread over ebony.
To novices who know so little how
A toughened log is split, who blundering
Excite derision with their futile swings
And glancing blows, he darts a look of pride;
And self content distends his large eyes wide.
What have we then that such a one can need?
The woods are his. He names each separate tree
And lives in intimacy such as we
Shall never know. The quietness is his,
The self sufficiency, and the raw strength. . . .

And for a moment this is quite enough
To see the quivering of a shapely helve
Pine white against the brown of last year's leaves
This is his day,—his day of secrets hid.

Oh, never hope to manage half as well! . . .
His firm black arms, bare to the shoulders, and
His well set, high powered body, all these tell
His mastery to him, as well to us.
A sculptor here could find the very model
From which to carve a statue setting forth
Health, Zest for Living, or whatever thing
Makes man persist in holding on to Faith.

This husky, blueclad oldster, shining black
With dull thick hair, and widened happy eyes
Sure of his prowess, has in his own way
Things to reveal. Watch how the lengthy swing
Of axe brings all the muscles into play;
Yet without haste, or waste, or rest.

We who

Belie ourselves in febrile gesturing
For praise, might learn from him, although we are wide.
He has done well what he was there to do.
Well, and with finish. There is nothing more.

Honey Mah Love

"Time is unsportsmanlike with us," I said.
"For all the cherished, lovely things we dreamed
Grow so much smaller than they ever seemed—"
And you, turned bitter, bowed your delicate head
Not soon enough to hide your eyes' dark pain.
For Time, old gambler, shrewd and sleight of hand
Had dealt us dull days for the golden days we planned.
And then we heard old Banjo Sam, astrummin' down the inky lane—
And the tinkling sounds came from his box as drops of silver sounding
   rain.

He sang:

    Wen de possum sets a eyein'
    De las' simmon on de tree
    I'll admit its sommut tryin'
    But it sho doan worry me—
        Case I doan mess wid trouble
        An trouble doan mess wid me
        Honey mah love
        I ain' no possum, see?

    When de whippoorwill's a cryin'
    In de lonely willer tree
    It might staht some po' boy sighin'
    But it sho doan worry me
        Case I doan mess wid trouble
        An trouble doan mess wid me
        Honey mah love
        I ain' no sad bird, see?

    When de brand new moon's adrippin'
    Yaller light on you an' me—
    Den mah heart, jes staht a skippin'
    An doan nothin' worry me
        Case I doan mess wid trouble
        An trouble doan mess wid me
        Honey mah love
        We ain' no derned fools, see?

We who have fretted our tired brains with fears
That time shall frustrate all our chosen dreams
We are rebuked by Banjo Sam's gay strains.
Oh Time may be less vicious than he seems;
And Troubles may grow weaker through the years—
Nearly as weak as those Sam told us of.—
Sam, strumming melodies to his honey love;
Sam, flouting Trouble in his inky lane.
Oh, I doan mess wid trouble. . . .

Dear child
Someday there will be truce from quarreling.
And someday all our silly fears will cease.
Someday there will be ways that we shall learn
To bilk old clandestine Time, and to return
His cheats, with one on him. Oh we shall bring
Someday to our ecstatic worshipping
More than our fretting fervor; something nearer peace,
Something near the surety we have been dreaming of.
Happy at last. . . . Oh happy! Honey, mah love. . . .

Memories of Salem

Lean pinchbeck housewives pointed their fingers,
Shrilled out their curses on youth and on beauty
Formed an implacable league
(Martyred defenders of Virtue and Duty!)
They with their lank hair and time flattened breasts
And stringy flesh tying their bones up so tightly
What could they do but intrigue
To silence the merriment rippling so lightly
From the ripe mouth of one, all too lovely and young—
Hating the songs that she sung
Hating the ground that she walked on.

Old snuffnosed parsons, spindleshanked, impotent,
Talked on, oh futilely, rabidly talked on
With psalmsinging voices stuck in their noses
Droned out their *"Vanity, vanity, vanity!"*
Having forgotten *(how could they remember)*
The wild winds of spring, and the fragrance of roses
Sodden themselves as a foggy November
Convinced at first hand of a worthless Humanity,
"Surely the girl is witchlike." (They spoke truth)
"Surely a girl so beautiful, lively
Leagues with the devil
Surely so musical a voice must be evil
(They with their sharp voices caught in their noses)
Surely her firm round breasts
Prithee cover them over!
Shall nurture the brats of old sin; oh, as surely
Shall pillow the head of an infidel lover
"Vanity of vanities; all is but vanity!"
(Even your platitudes, Reverend Fool!)

Thus in the old straitlaced days did the Parsons
Cry out on 'witches' and ironclad housewives

Wild with unspeakable wrath did insanely
Clamor for vengeance on any wild beauties
Living their happier lives. . . .

    . . .

What is the wonder
That we today on their chocked Sunday mornings
Laugh at the churchgoers frowning and whispering
(Who killed off our parents but could not kill us)
And our laughter is vengeance enough for us two
And vengeance enough that we seek (while they finger
Their prayerbooks, their pennies) the spring attend open
The rose scented woodland—where lying at peace
On some hidden hill, far from crabbed age and gossip
My ragged head pillowed soft on your bosom—
Oh drowning in the sunshine that streaks the deep auburn
Mass of your loosened hair—what could we do
Other than seek us our own magic worship
In our own way—to divulge wizardries
As we know best. . . . our laughter more musical
Than angry churchbells, clanking the distance,
Remonstrant, absurd—
Than the voice of a parson
Bellowing like a foghorn, lost in heavy fog?

Idyll

I found me a cranny of perpetual dusk.
There for the grateful sense was pungent musk
Of rotting leaves, and moss, mingled with scents
Of heavy clusters freighting foxgrape vines.
The sun was barred except at close of day
When he could weakly etch in changing lines
A filigree upon the silver trunks
Of maple and of poplar. There were oaks
Their black bark fungus-spotted, and there lay
An old wormeaten segment of gray fence
Tumbling in consonant long forgot decay.
Motionless the place save when a little wind
Rippled the leaves, and soundless too it was
Save for a stream nearly inaudible,
That made a short stay in closewoven grass
Then in elusive whispers bade farewell;
Save for the noise of birds, whistling security.

One afternoon I lay there drowsily
Steeped in the crannies' love benevolence;
Peaceful the far dreams I was dreaming of. . . .
Sharply a stranger whistle screeched above
Once then again. Nearly as suddenly
A hawk dove, swooping past the sagging fence
Past a short shrub, and like a heavy rock
Striking the ground. I started up, the hawk
Flew off unhurriedly with fine insolence,
On vigorous wings, and settled on the limb
Of a dead chestnut. His sentinel mate
Screeched down another cry, almost too late.

On the matting of the leaves, a small bird lay
Spattering blood and on the little stream
A fluff of blue feathers floated away.
The hawk awhile gazed at me, I at him—
Splendid the corsair's breast and head of white
And dauntless, daring poise. Then with a cry
Frustrate, vindictive, he wheeled in graceful flight.
The wind stirred faintly, there was nothing more
Of sound, except a snatch of woodland song
As earlier. The stream purred listlessly along,
And all grew quite as peaceful as before.

One Way of Taking Leave

We knew, the coming day would see us parted
After our too brief Eden, for too long—
Oh we, so wise, so wise and brokenhearted—
So pitiful, and so absurdly strong, . . .
Therefore we rushed out, lest the wellknown room
Should wall us in with the old futility;—
And tramped strange streets, where dimly, in the gloom
Huddled poor witches—no wretcheder than we.

The wan tired light crept in the livid skies,
And we turned homeward, turning from the light,
Bitter our unsaid words, empty our eyes, . . .
We met the working people on the stair,
Who gazed askance at that 'same madcap pair'
Their light eyebrows saying 'A wild, wild night'. . . .

Isaiah To Mandy

Oh de wagon keeps a rollin'
    All de sisters sing
  An de hammers keeps a knockin'
    An' de bells all ring—

An de preacher keeps a preachin'
    Dat muh time come too
But he ain't let out no 'pinion
    Dat I'll be wid you—

Oh dey say I'll see de angels
    All a floppin roun de place
Dey don' tell me of no angel
    Wid yo brownskin face

But I knows no wings kin ca'y
    Any folks aroun
Mo lively dan yo' struttin
    When de Charleston soun'

Dey'll be tinklin brass and cymbal
    An de guitar too
I don't want no music p'tikler
    Thout I dance wid you

An' de vittels dey is righteous
    An' de drinkins fine dey say
Well, I ain't so hungry, honey
    Not so ve'y dat away

Oh dis heaven dey all promises
    An jes talks an talks about
Mought be fine fo dem as needs it
    But, guess I kin do widout

All de eatin' an de drinkin'
    An de shoutin' song
Don' min dyin; honey
    But gotta stay too very long

Conjured

"She done put huh little hands
On the back uh my head;
I cain't git away from her
Twill I'm dead.

"She done laid her little body
Beneaf my breast,
And I won't never
Git no rest.

"She done been in my arms
Twill the break of day
Won't never
Git away. . . .

"She done put her little shoes
Underneaf my bed
Never git away from her
Twill I'm dead.

"Won't want to leave her
Then," he said.
"Oh, baby, gotta lay
So long
Alone. . . ."

Long Track Blues

Went down to the yards
To see the signal lights come on;
Looked down the track
Where my lovin' babe done gone.

Red light in my block,
Green light down the line;
Lawdy, let yo' green light
Shine down on that babe o' mine.

Heard a train callin'
Blowin' long ways down the track;
Ain't no train due here,
Baby, what can bring you back?

Brakeman tell me
Got a powerful ways to go;
He don't know my feelin's
Baby, when he's talkin' so.

Lanterns a-swingin',
An' a long freight leaves the yard;
Leaves me here, baby,
But my heart it rides de rod.

Sparks a flyin',
Wheels rumblin' wid a mighty roar;
Then the red tail light,
And the place gets dark once more.

Dog in the freight room
Howlin' like he los' his mind;
Might howl myself,
If I was the howlin' kind.

Norfolk and Western,
Baby, and the C. & O.;
How come they treat
A hardluck feller so?

Red light in my block,
Green light down the line;
Lawdy, let yo' green light
Shine down on that babe o' mine.

An Annotated Bibliography of the Works of Sterling A. Brown

by Robert G. O'Meally

Sterling A. Brown is a distinguished writer whose poems, short stories, reviews, and scholarly works have appeared for more than fifty years. His poetry reflects the innovative impulse of contemporary verse as well as the toughness, humor, and protest of black American folklore. And his reportorial narratives and sketches of the Southern scene are alive with black talk, and they convey vividly the terror and the irony of "living Jim Crow" during the forties. Brown has studied the role of blacks in American folklore, literature, and music since the New Negro Renaissance period. His work also has provided perspective to *New* New Negroes, including Black Aesthetic writers of the sixties and seventies.

This annotated bibliography, arranged according to subject and date of publication, is designed to assist readers in locating Brown's works, many of which are uncollected or out of print.

For assisting me in tracking down materials, I am indebted to Cornelia Stokes and Ahmos Zu-Bolton at Founder's Library, Howard University. Special thanks go to Sterling A. Brown, teacher, hero, friend.

I. POEMS

A. Poems included in SOUTHERN ROAD, but published previously:

"Challenge," "Odyssey of Big Boy," "Return," "Salutamus," "To a Certain Lady, in Her Garden." *Caroling Dusk.* Edited by Countee Cullen. New York: Harper and Brothers, 1927, pp. 130–139.

"Foreclosure." *Ebony and Topaz, A Collectanea.* Edited by Charles S. Johnson. New York: *Opportunity, Journal of Negro Life,* [1] 1927, p. 36.

"Old Man Buzzard." *The Carolina Magazine,* LVIII (May, 1927), 25–26.

"When de Saints Go Ma'ching Home." *Opportunity,* V (July, 1927), 48.

"Thoughts of Death." *Opportunity,* VI (August 6, 1928), 242.

"Long Gone." *Anthology of Negro American Literature.* Edited by V. F. Calverton. New York: Modern Library, 1929, pp. 209–210.

"Riverbank Blues." *Opportunity,* VII (May, 1929), 148.

---

[1] Hereafter, *Opportunity, Journal of Negro Life* will be cited as *Opportunity.*

"Effie." *Opportunity,* VII (October, 1929), 304.

"Dark of the Moon," "Ma Rainey," "Southern Road." *Folk-Say, a Regional Miscellany,*[2] II. Edited by Benjamin A. Botkin. Norman, Oklahoma: University of Oklahoma Press, 1930, pp. 275–279.

"Memphis Blues," "Slim Greer," "Strong Men." *The Book of American Negro Poetry.* Edited by James Weldon Johnson. New York: Harcourt, Brace, 1931, pp. 248–266.

"Convict," "New St. Louis Blues," "Old King Cotton," "Pardners," "Revelations," "Slow Coon" (later published as "Slim Lands a Job"), "Tin Roof Blues." *Folk-Say,* III. Edited by Benjamin A. Botkin. Norman, Oklahoma: Oklahoma Folklore Society, 1931, pp. 113–123.

B. SOUTHERN ROAD. New York: Harcourt, Brace, 1932.
Brown's first book of poems.

C. Poems not in SOUTHERN ROAD:

"After the Storm." *The Crisis, a Record of the Darker Races,*[3] XXXIV (April, 1927), 48.

"A Bad, Bad Man," "Call Boy," "Long Track Blues," "Puttin' on Dog," "Rent Day Blues," "Slim in Hell." *Folk-Say,* IV. Edited by Benjamin A. Botkin. Norman, Oklahoma: Oklahoma Folklore Society, 1932, pp. 249–256.

"He Was a Man." *Opportunity,* X (June, 1932), 179.

"Let Us Suppose." *Opportunity,* XIII (September, 1935), 281.

"Southern Cop," "Transfer." *Partisan Review,* III (October, 1936), 220–221.

"Master and Man." *New Republic,* LXXXIX (November 18, 1936), 66.

"All Are Gay." *American Stuff.* New York: Viking Press, 1937, pp. 79–81.

"Break of Day." *New Republic,* LXXXV (May 11, 1938), 10.

"The Young Ones." *Poetry,* III (July, 1938), 189–190.

"Glory, Glory." *Esquire,* X (August, 1938), 78.

"Colloquy (Black Worker and White Worker)," "Conjured," "Old Lem." *This Generation.* Edited by George Anderson and Eda L. Walton. New York: Scott, Foresman, 1939, pp. 645–646.

"Sharecropper." *Get Organized.* Edited by Alan Calmer. New York: International Press, 1939, pp. 24–25.

"Bitter Fruit of the Tree." *The Nation,* CXLIX (August 26, 1939), 223.

"Remembering Nat Turner." *The Crisis,* XLVI (February, 1939), 48.

"An Old Woman Remembers," "The Ballad of Joe Meek." *Freedomways,* III (Summer, 1963), 405–411.

These poems, according to a headnote, were "written over a score of years ago."

"Crispus Attucks McCoy." *Ik Ben de Nieuwe Neger.* Edited by Rosie Pool. Den Haag: B. Dakker, 1965, p. 49.

---

[2]Hereafter, *Folk-Say, a Regional Miscellany* will be cited as *Folk-Say.*
[3]Hereafter, *The Crisis, a Record of the Darker Races* will be cited as *The Crisis.*

D. THE LAST RIDE OF WILD BILL AND ELEVEN NARRATIVE POEMS. Detroit: Broadside Press, 1975.

Collection of ballads, including previously unpublished poems, "The Last Ride of Wild Bill" and "Slim Hears the Call"; "Sam Smiley" from *Southern Road* appears here as "Sam Yancy."

II. NARRATIVES AND SKETCHES

"Out of Their Mouths." *Survey Graphic,* XXI (November, 1942), 480–483.

Anecdotes, conversations, statements by black and white Americans on race relations.

"Words on a Bus." *South Today,* VII (Spring, 1943), 26–28.

Narrative about a black man who flirts with a black woman on a segregated bus.

"Farewell to Basin Street." *The Record Changer,* III (December, 1944), 7–9, 51.

Sketch in which a first-person narrator recalls a trip to New Orleans, which he found more of a monument to the past than a thriving jazz center.

"The Muted South." *Phylon, the Atlanta University Review of Race and Culture,* [4] VI (Winter, 1945), 22–34.

Five sketches of the South dealing with racism and the war as well as black American life styles and folk art forms.

"Georgia Sketches." *Phylon,* VI (Summer, 1945), 225–231.

Two sketches of Atlanta: one dealing with two blacks' attempt to visit Joel Chandler Harris's home, the other consisting of recollections of public jazz dances.

"Georgia Nymphs." *Phylon,* VI (Autumn, 1945), 362–367.

Sketch about two black men who happen upon bathing white women; the men leave town with caution and haste.

"And/Or." *Phylon,* VII (Fall, 1946), 269–272.

Narrative focusing upon a black collegiate's struggles to vote in segregated Alabama.

III. BOOKS OF CRITICISM

Outline for the Study of the Poetry of American Negroes. New York: Harcourt, Brace, 1931.

Supplement to James Weldon Johnson's anthology, *The Book of American Negro Poetry;* includes topics for papers, study questions, definitions of poetic forms and elements, and an essay on contemporary American verse.

[4] Hereafter, *Phylon, the Atlanta University Review of Race and Culture* will be cited as *Phylon.*

The Negro in American Fiction. Washington: Associates in Negro Folk Education, 1938.

Critical essays on the portrayal of blacks in American fiction.

Negro Poetry and Drama. Washington: Associates in Negro Folk Education, 1938.

Critical history of black American poetry and drama.

The Negro Caravan. Edited by Sterling A. Brown, Arthur P. Davis, and Ulysses Lee. New York: Dryden Press, 1941.

Anthology of Afro-American writing from its folk foundations to 1940; includes critical and historical interchapters by the editors.

The Reader's Companion to World Literature. Edited by Lillian H. Hornstein and G. D. Percy. New York: New American Library, 1956.

Dictionary of international writers and their major works; Brown contributed entries on Matthew Arnold, Charles Baudelaire, Emily Brontë, Robert Burns, Emily Dickinson. Ralph Waldo Emerson, Benjamin Franklin, Robert Frost, Heinrich Heine, A. E. Housman, Thomas Jefferson, Abraham Lincoln, Henry Wadsworth Longfellow, Herman Melville, *Moby Dick,* Edgar Allan Poe, Henry Thoreau, Mark Twain, and Walt Whitman.

IV. ESSAYS ON AMERICAN LITERATURE AND THE ROLE OF BLACKS IN AMERICAN LITERATURE

"Negro Literature—Is It True? Complete?" *The Durham Fact-Finding Conference,* Durham, North Carolina: Fact-Finding Conference, 1929, pp. 26–28.

Statement in defense of realism in the portrayal of blacks in literature.

"Our Literary Audience." *Opportunity,* VIII (February, 1930), 42–46, 61.

Criticism of readers who are put off by realistic portraiture of Negroes in literature.

"James Weldon Johnson." *The Book of American Negro Poetry.* Edited by James Weldon Johnson. New York: Harcourt, Brace, 1931, pp. 114–117.

Biographical headnote preceding the selection of Johnson's poetry.

"A Literary Parallel." *Opportunity,* X (May, 1932), 152–153.

Discussion of stereotypes in fiction and drama: English, Irish, American.

"In Memoriam: Charles W. Chesnutt." *Opportunity,* X (December, 1932), 387.

Eulogy of Chesnutt and evaluation of his stories and novels.

"Negro Character As Seen by White Authors." *The Journal of Negro Education,* II (April, 1933), 179–203.

Discussion of black stereotypes in American literature of the nineteenth and twentieth centuries; a few true portraits, "realizations," also noted.

"Problems of the Negro Writer." *Official Proceedings, National Negro Congress.* Washington: National Negro Congress Publications, 1937, pp. 18–19.

Transcript of a speech advocating techniques and perspectives of realism in black writing.

"The Negro in American Literature." *James Weldon Johnson, a Biographical Sketch.* Nashville: Fisk University, 1938, pp. 20–28.

Transcript of a speech surveying black literature; the contributions of Johnson are highlighted.

"The American Race Problem as Reflected in American Literature." *The Journal of Negro Education,* VIII (July, 1939), 275–290.

Study of racial attitudes expressed in American writing of the nineteenth and twentieth centuries.

"The Negro Writer and His Publisher." *The Quarterly Review of Higher Education Among Negroes,* IX (July, 1941), 140–146.

Discussion of the problems black writers face getting published, stressing their responsibility to practice their craft without excuse or compromise.

"Negro in the American Theatre." *Oxford Companion to the Theatre.* Edited by Phyllis Hartnoll. London: Oxford Press, 1950, pp. 672–679.

Essay surveying the contributions of Afro-American actors and playwrights to American theatre from the colonial period to 1947.

"In the American Grain." *Vassar Alumnae Magazine,* XXXVI (February, 1951), pp. 5–9.

Essay tracing realism in American literature, from Emerson to Faulkner.

"Seventy-five Years of the Negro in Literature." *Jackson College Bulletin,* II (September, 1953), 26–30.

Transcribed address at Jackson College, outlining American writers' uses and abuses of black folklore.

"The New Negro in Literature (1925–1955)." *The New Negro Thirty Years Afterwards.* Washington: Howard University Press, 1955.

Transcript of a speech surveying American literature (1925–1955) by and about blacks.

"A Century of Negro Portraiture in American Literature." *The Massachusetts Review,* VII (Winter, 1966), 73–96.

Essay on the treatment of racial themes and black characters in Post-Civil War literature.

"Arna Bontemps, Co-Worker, Comrade," *Black World,* XXII (September, 1973), 11, 91–97.

Eulogy of Bontemps and appraisal of his writings.

V. ESSAYS AND COMMENTARIES ON BLACK FOLKLORE AND MUSIC

"Roland Hayes," *Opportunity*, III, 30 (June, 1925), pp. 173–174.

Brown's first published writing, an award-winning sketch of the renowned tenor.

"The Blues as Folk Poetry." *Folk-Say*, I. Edited by Benjamin A. Botkin. Norman, Oklahoma: University of Oklahoma Press, 1930, pp. 324–339.

Discussion of the forms and meanings of blues songs

"The Folk Roots." *Vanguard* LP—VSD—47/48. Liner notes. Copyright 1973.

Excerpt from a speech on the blues given at the "Spirituals to Swing" concert at Carnegie Hall, December 24, 1939.

"Blues, Ballads and Social Songs." *Seventy-five Years of Freedom*. Washington: Library of Congress Press, December 18, 1940, pp. 17–25.

Discussion of the meaning and "mood" of Afro-American folk music.

"The Negro in American Culture." Unpublished memoranda, Carnegie/Myrdal study of blacks in America, 1940.

Survey of the contributions of blacks to American theatre, music, and sports.

"Stray Notes on Jazz." *Vassar Brew*, XXVII (June, 1946), 15–19.

Discussion of the influence of recording companies on jazz.

"Remarks at a Conference on the Character and State of Studies in Folklore." *Journal of American Folklore*, LIX (October, 1946), 506–507.

Transcript of Brown's speech on folklore, "living-people-lore," as important to artists, folklorists, and historians.

"Negro Folk Expression." *Phylon*, XI (Autumn, 1950), 318–327.

Analysis of the origins and meanings of Afro-American jokes and tales.

"Athletics and the Arts." *Integration of the Negro into American Society*. Edited by E. Franklin Frazier. Washington: Howard University Press, 1951, 117–147.

Discussion of the struggles for integration by blacks in literature, art, music, dance, and sports.

"The Blues." *Phylon*, XIII (Autumn, 1952), 286–292.

Paper read at the "Post-Tanglewood Round Table on Jazz," Lenox, Massachusetts, August, 1952; deals with the underlying themes and the poetry of the blues.

"Negro Folk Expression: Spirituals, Seculars, Ballads and Work Songs." *Phylon*, XIV (Winter, 1953), 45–61.

Essay on the history, meanings, and poetic elements in the folk songs of Afro-Americans.

"Portrait of a Jazz Giant: 'Jelly Roll' Morton (1885?–1941)." *Black World*, XXIII (February, 1974), 28–49.

Essay on Morton's importance as composer, pianist, and singer.

VI. REVIEWS AND NOTES ON BOOKS, MOVIES, PLAYS

"Two African Heroines" *Opportunity*, IV (January, 1926), 24–26.

Review of David Garnett's novel, *The Sailor's Return*, and Louis Charbonneau's novel, *Mambu, et Son Amour*.

"The New Secession—a Review." *Opportunity*, V (May, 1927), 147–148.

Review of Julia Peterkin's novel, *Black April*.

"Our Book Shelf." *Opportunity*, VI (March, 1928), 91–92.

Review of *Dwellers in the Jungle*, a novel by Gordon Casserly.

"Fabulist and Felossofer." *Opportunity*, VI (July, 1928), 211–212.

Review of *Ol' Man Adam an' His Chillun*, a novel by Roark Bradford.

"Mamba's Daughters." *Opportunity*, VII (May, 1929), 161–162.

A review of DuBose Heyward's novel, *Mamba's Daughters*.

"Black Ulysses at War." *Opportunity*, VII (December, 1929), 383–384.

Review of *Wings on My Feet*, a novel by Howard Odum.

"Unhistoric History." *Journal of Negro History*, XV (April, 1930), 134–161.

Essay on historical fiction and biography focusing on *Quiet Cities* and *Swords and Roses*, novels by Joseph Hergesheimer; *Stonewall Jackson* and *Jefferson Davis*, biographies by Allen Tate; *John Brown*, a biography by Robert Penn Warren; *Abraham Lincoln*, a biography by Raymond Holden; and *The Tragic Era*, a novel by Claude Bowers.

"Not Without Laughter," *Opportunity*, VIII (September, 1930), 279–280.

Review of *Not Without Laughter*, a novel by Langston Hughes.

"Black Genesis." *Opportunity*, VIII (October, 1930), 311–312.

Review of *Black Genesis*, a collection of stories by Samuel G. Stoney and Gertrude M. Shelby.

"Chronicle and Comment." *Opportunity*, VIII (December, 1930), 375.

Notes on literary and scholarly works by Abram Harris, Carter Woodson, Geroge Schuyler, and Randolph Edmonds.

"Folk Values in a New Medium." Co-author, Alain Locke. *Folk-Say*, II. Edited by Benjamin A. Botkin. Norman, Oklahoma: University of Oklahoma Press, 1930, pp. 340–345.

Review of two movies, "Hearts in Dixie" and "Hallelujah."

"The Literary Scene." *Opportunity*, IX (January, 1931), 20.

Notes on *Folk-Say* II, an annual collection of folklore materials, edited by Benjamin A. Botkin; *Short History of Julia*, a novel by Isa Glen; *Po' Buckra*, a novel by Samuel G. Stoney and Gertrude M. Shelby; *Gulf Stream*, a novel by Marie Stanley; *Strike!* a novel by Mary Vorse; and essays and poems by Carl Carmer.

"The Literary Scene." *Opportunity*, IX (February, 1931), 53–54.

Notes on *The Black Worker*, a study of the relation of blacks to the American labor movement, by Abram Harris and Sterling Spero, and *Black No More*, a novel by George Schuyler.

"The Literary Scene, Chronicle and Commentary." *Opportunity*, IX (March, 1931), 87.

Notes on many books, including the scholarly works, *Race Psychology* by Thomas R. Garth, and *The Negro Wage Earner* by Lorenzo Greene, a novel, *Jungle Ways* by William Seabrook; and a collection of short stories, *Golden Tales from the South*, edited by May Becker.

"A Romantic Defense." *Opportunity*, IX (April, 1931), 118.

Review of *I'll Take My Stand*, a collection of essays by Twelve Southerners.

"An American Epoch." *Opportunity*, IX (June, 1931), 187.

Review of Howard Odum's novel, *An American Epoch, Southern Portraiture in the National Picture.*

"Our Bookshelf." *Opportunity*, IX (June, 1931), 199.

Review of Arna Bontemps's novel, *God Sends Sunday.*

"As to 'Jungle Ways.'" *Opportunity*, IX (July, 1931), 219–221.

Review of John Seabrook's novel, *Jungle Ways.*

"Caroling Softly Souls of Slavery." *Opportunity*, IX (August, 1931), 241–252.

Commentary on Louis C. Hughes's autobiography, *Thirty Years a Slave.*

"Concerning Negro Drama." *Opportunity*, IX (September, 1931), 284–288.

Comments on "The Green Pastures," "The Emperor Jones," and other plays of black life by white playwrights.

"Poor Whites." *Opportunity*, IX (October, 1931), 317, 320.

Review of Erskine Caldwell's collection of stories, *American Earth;* John Fort's novel, *God in the Straw Pen;* and Geroge Millburn's novel, *Oklahoma Town.*

"The Point of View." *Opportunity*, IX (November, 1931), 347–350.

Discussion of "point of view" in literature with reference to Elizabethan drama, American minstrelsy, black folklore, and the fiction of William Faulkner, Roark Bradford, and DuBose Heyward.

"Pride and Pathos." *Opportunity*, IX (December, 1931), 381–384.

Review of *The Carolina Low Country*, a collection of essays by Members of the Society for the Preservation of the Spirituals.

"Never No Steel Driving Man." *Opportunity*, IX (December, 1931), 382.

Review of *John Henry*, a novel by Roark Bradford.

"Truth Will Out." *Opportunity*, X (January, 1932), 23–24.

Review of Frederic Bancroft's *Slave Trading in the Old South*, a history.

"'Never No More.'" *Opportunity*, X (February, 1932), 55–56.

Review of James Millen's play, "Never No More."

"Weep Some More My Lady." *Opportunity*, X (March, 1932), 87.

Comments on Louis Untermeyer's presentation of black folklore in his anthology, *American Poetry: From the Beginning to Whitman.*

"Joel Chandler Harris." *Opportunity*, X (April, 1932), 119–120.

Review of *Joel Chandler Harris: Editor* and *Essayist, a* collection of Harris's essays, edited by Julia Collier Harris.

"More Odds." *Opportunity,* X (June, 1932), pp. 188–189.

Review of Edwin Embree's *Brown America,* a social history of blacks in America.

"Local Color or Interpretation." *Opportunity,* X (July, 1932), 223.

Review of Julia Peterkin's novel, *Bright Skin.*

"A Poet and His Prose." *Opportunity,* X (August, 1932), 256.

Commentary on Claude McKay's novels and stories.

"Signs of Promise." *Opportunity,* X (September, 1932), 287.

Comments on *University of Michigan Plays,* an anthology edited by Kenneth T. Rowe.

"Amber Satyr." *Opportunity,* X (November, 1932), 352.

Review of Roy Flannagan's novel, *Amber Satyr.*

"A New Trend." *Opportunity,* XI (February, 1933), 56.

Comments on *Inchin' Along,* a novel by Welbourne Kelley, as well as *Free Born* and *Georgia Nigger,* novels by John L. Spivak.

"Alas the Poor Mulatto." *Opportunity,* XI (March, 1933), 91.

Review of *Dark Lustre,* a novel by Geoffrey Barnes.

"Time for a New Deal." *Opportunity,* II (April, 1933), 122, 126.

Review of *The Southern Oligarchy,* a study of the politics and economics of the American South by William Scaggs.

"Smartness Goes Traveling." *Opportunity,* XI (May, 1933), 154, 158.

Review of Evelyn Waugh's narrative of travels in Africa, *They Were Still Dancing,* and his novel, *Black Mischief.*

"John Brown: God's Angry Man." *Opportunity,* XI (June, 1933), 186–187.

Review of *God's Angry Man,* a biography of John Brown by Leonard Ehrlick.

"Banana Bottom." *Opportunity,* XI (July, 1933), 217, 222.

Review of Claude McKay's novel, *Banana Bottom.*

"From the Southwest." *Opportunity,* XI (October, 1933), 313.

Review of *Negrito,* a novel by J. Mason Brewer, and *Tone the Bell Easy,* a journal of folklore studies, edited by J. Frank Dobie.

"Kingdom Coming." *Opportunity,* XI (December, 1933), 382–383.

Review of Roark Bradford's novel, *Kingdom Coming.*

"Arcadia, South Carolina." *Opportunity,* XII (February, 1934), 59–60.

Review of *Roll, Jordan, Roll,* a narrative history and pictorial essay on black Americans, by Doris Ulmann and Julia Peterkin.

"Satire of Imperialism" *Opportunity,* XII (March, 1934), 89–90.

Review of Winifred Holtby's novel, *Mandos, Mandos!*

"Six Plays for a Negro Theatre." *Opportunity,* XII (September, 1934), 280–281.

Review of Six Plays for a Negro Theatre," a collection of Randolph Edmond's plays.

"The Atlanta Summer Theatre." *Opportunity,* XII (October, 1934), 308–309.

Commentary on Atlanta University's five dramatic productions, summer, 1934.

"Stars Fell on Alabama." *Opportunity,* XII (October, 1934), 312–313.
Review of Carl Carmer's novel, *Stars Fell on Alabama.*

"Mississippi—Old Style." *Opportunity,* XII (December, 1934), 377–378.
Review of *So Red the Rose,* a novel by Stark Young.

"Mississippi, Alabama: New Style." *Opportunity,* XIII (February, 1935), 55–56.
Commentary on Southern novels by Thomas Wolfe, William March, and T. S. Stribling.

"The Negro in Fiction and Drama." *The Christian Register,* CXIV (February 14, 1935), 111–112.
Review of fiction by Stark Young, William March, T. S. Stribling, Zora Neale Hurston, and Langston Hughes.

"Imitation of Life: Once a Pancake." *Opportunity,* XIII (March, 1935), 87–88.
Review of *Imitation of Life,* a novel by Fannie Hurst.

"Mr. Sterling Brown." *Opportunity,* XIII (April, 1935), 121–122.
Reply to Fannie Hurst's objections to the review of *Imitation of Life.*

"Correspondence." *Opportunity,* XIII (May, 1935), 153.
Response to a letter to the editor about "Imitation of Life: Once a Pancake" and *Southern Road.*

"Come Day, Go Day." *Opportunity,* XIII (September, 1935), 279–280.
Review of Roark Bradford's collection of short stories, *Let the Band Play Dixie,* and Richard Coleman's novel, *Don't You Weep, Don't You Moan.*

"Realism in the South." *Opportunity,* XIII (October, 1935), 311–312.
Review of *Kneel to the Rising Sun,* a collection of short stories by Erskine Caldwell, and *Deep Dark River,* a novel by Robert Rylee.

"Southern Cross Sections." *Opportunity,* XIII (December, 1935), 380–385.
Review of *Siesta,* a novel by Barry Fleming, and *South,* a novel by Frederick Wright.

"Shadow of the Plantation." *Journal of Negro History,* XXI (January, 1936), 70–73.
Review of Charles S. Johnson's sociological study, *Shadow of the Plantation.*

"The First Negro Writers." *The New Republic,* LXXXVI (May 6, 1936) 376–377.
Review of Benjamin Brawley's anthology, *Early Negro Writers.*

"Two Negro Poets." *Opportunity,* XIV (July, 1936), 216–220.
Review of *Black Thunder,* a historical novel by Arna Bontemps, and *Black Man's Verse,* a collection of poems by Frank Marshall Davis.

"Book Reviews." *Opportunity,* XV (September, 1937), 280–281.
Review of *The Negro Genius* essays on black artists and intellectuals, by Benjamin Brawley.

"Biography." *Opportunity*, XV (September, 1937), 216–217.

   Appraisal of Benjamin Brawley's *Paul Laurence Dunbar, Poet of His People*, a biography.

" 'Luck is a Fortune.' " *The Nation*, CXLV (October 16, 1937), 409–410.

   Review of Zora Neale Hurston's novel, *Their Eyes Were Watching God*.

"Prize Winning Stories." *Opportunity*, XVI (April, 1938), 120–121.

   Review of *Uncle Tom's Children*, Richard Wright's collection of stories.

"From the Inside." *The Nation*, CLXVI (April 16, 1938), 448.

   Review of *Uncle Tom's Children*, Richard Wright's collection of stories.

"South on the Move." *Opportunity*, XVI (December, 1938), 366–369.

   Review of *A Southerner Discovers the South*, a travel book by Jonathan Daniels, and *Forty Acres and Steel Mules*, an economist's portrait of the South by Herman Clarence Nixon.

"Insight, Courage, and Craftsmanship." *Opportunity*, XVIII (June, 1940), 185–186.

   Review of Richard Wright's novel, *Native Son*.

"Forward." *Place: America*, a play by Thomas Richardson. New York: NAACP Press, 1940, pp. 4–5.

   Introductory note, recommending this play.

"Three Ways of Looking at the South." *Journal of Negro Education*, XIV (Winter, 1945), 68–72.

   Review of William Percy's autobiography, *Lanterns on the Levee;* Anne Walker's study of Tuskegee Institute and town, *Tuskegee and the Black Belt;* and Ira De A. Reid's discussion of tenant farmers, *Sharecroppers All*.

VII. ON RECORD AND TAPE

"Readings by Sterling Brown and Langston Hughes." *Folkways* LP—FP90. Copyright 1952.

   Recitation by Brown of "Break of Day," "Old King Cotton," "Old Lem," "Puttin' on Dog," "Sharecropper," "Slim in Hell."

"Anthology of Negro Poets, Edited by Arna Bontemps." *Folkways* LP—FL 9791. Copyright 1966.

   Recitation by Brown of "Long Gone" and "Ma Rainey."

"Sixteen Poems of Sterling A. Brown." *Folkways* LP—FL 9794 Copyright 1978.

   Recitation by Brown of poems published in *Southern Road* and in periodicals; also, "Cloteel," "Parish Doctor," and "Uncle Joe" are presented here for the first time.

"Sterling Brown." Interview by Steven Jones. On file at the Institute for Arts and Humanities and the Afro-American Resource Center, Howard University, May 4, 14, 1978.

Tape recorded interview at Brown's home concerning the poet's early years in Washington, D. C.

"Sterling Brown Lectures." On file at the Institute for Arts and Humanities and the Afro-American Resource Center, Howard University, September 19 and October 10, 17, 31, 1973.

"Sterling Brown." Interview by Dyalsingh Sadhi. On file at the Institute for Arts and Humanities and the Afro-American Resource Center, Howard University, January 10, 1974.

Videotaped interview at Howard University concerning Brown's years at Lincoln University.

"Sterling Brown Poetry Recital." On file at the Institute for Arts and Humanities and the Afro-American Resource Center, Howard University, May 17, 1974.

Speech by Brown at the M. L. King Library, Washington, D.C., about the influences on his poetry; a reading of seventeen published poems.

VIII. MISCELLANEOUS

"The Negro in Washington." *Washington: City and Capital.* Federal Writers' Project. Washington: Government Printing Office, 1937.

Collection of essays by Brown dealing with the political and cultural history of black Washingtonians.

The Negro in Virginia. Writers' Project. New York: Hastings House, 1940.

Collection of essays on the history and folklore of blacks in Virginia. Although as Federal Writers' Project Editor for Negro Affairs (1936–1940) Brown helped edit virtually every Project essay dealing with black life, he worked most extensively on *The Negro in Virginia,* even writing entire sections himself.

"Poetry Corner." Mary Strong. *Scholastic,* XXXVI (April 29, 1940), 25, 27.

Strong's discussion of Brown's life and poetry includes lengthy statements by the poet himself.

"Saving the Cargo (Sidelights on the Underground Railroad)." *The Negro History Bulletin,* IV (April, 1941), 151–154.

Historical essay on the trials of Underground Railroad conductors and riders.

"The Contributions of the American Negro." *One America.* Edited by Frances Brown and Joseph Roucek. New York: Prentice-Hall, 1945, pp. 588–615.

Essay surveying the Negro's contributions to American political and cultural history.

"Count Us In." *Primer for White Folks.* Edited by Bucklin Moon. Garden City: Doubleday, 1945, pp. 364–395.

    Essay on segregation and prejudice, with focus on the black serviceman.

Ralph Bunche—Statesman." *The Reporter,* I (December 6, 1949), 3–6.

    Biographical sketch.

"Negro, American." By Sterling A. Brown, John Hope Franklin, and Rayford Logan. *Encyclopædia Britannica,* XVI, Chicago: William Benton, 1968, pp. 188–201.

    Essay on the role of blacks in American life, from slavery through the mid-1960s.

"The Teacher . . . Sterling Brown, The Mentor of Thousands . . . Talks About Art, Black and White." Sterling A. Brown and Hollie West. *The Washington Post,* CXIII, 346 (November 16, 1969), pp. F1–F3.

    Interview dealing with black folklore, music, and the relation of blacks and whites.

"Appendixes." *The American Slave: From Sunup to Sundown.* Edited by George Rawick. Westport, Connecticut: Greenwood, 1972, pp. 172–178.

    Outlining certain WPA procedures for interviewing ex-slaves, these official memoranda (1937) were influenced by the Project's Editor for Negro Affairs, Sterling Brown.

"Sterling Brown, a Living Legend." Genevieve Ekaete. *New Directions,* I (Winter, 1974), 4–11.

    Tribute by Ekaete, containing statements by Brown on culture and politics.

"A Son's Return: 'Oh Didn't He Ramble.' " *Berkshire Review,* X (Summer, 1974), 9–30.

    Transcript of a talk in which Brown recalls his student years at Williams College.

"Blacks in Brookland." *The Washington Star* (April 18, 1979), A-17.

    Letter to the Editor defending Brown's neighborhood in Washington as something more than a "ghetto."

About the Author

Sterling Allen Brown, one of America's most influential poets and scholars, was born in Washington, D.C., in 1901. His father was the Reverend Sterling N. Brown, a graduate of Fisk University and Oberlin College, an author, and professor of religion at Howard University. Sterling A. Brown attended Dunbar High School, where he edited a magazine and began writing poetry. Among his schoolmates were Mercer Cook, once ambassador to Senegal; W. Allison Davis, John Dewey Professor of Education, University of Chicago; the late William Hastie, federal judge; and W. Montague Cobb, the distinguished anthropologist.

Brown enrolled in Williams College in 1918, graduating Phi Beta Kappa. In 1923 he took his master's degree at Harvard University. Brown's first nationally published essay, on Roland Hayes, won a prize in the *Opportunity* magazine contest sponsored by the Urban League. This was 1925, the era of far-reaching literary activity known as the Harlem Renaissance, which brought fame to such writers as Zora Neale Hurston, Langston Hughes, and Countee Cullen.

Brown's legendary career as a teacher began during this period. He taught at the Virginia Seminary and College from 1926 to 1928, where he met his wife, Daisy Turnbull, and then at Fisk University. He also taught at Lincoln University in Missouri and Atlanta University. It was in the South that Brown developed his extraordinary understanding of Afro-American folklore which is a distinguishing feature of his most famous poems. In 1929, Brown joined the faculty of Howard University, an institution with which he has been associated for more than half a century.

The year Brown enrolled in the doctoral program at Harvard his first book, *Outline for the Study of the Poetry of American Negroes,* was issued, designed to be used in conjunction with James Weldon Johnson's *The Book of American Negro Poetry.* Brown's first volume of poetry, the highly acclaimed *Southern Road,* was published in 1932.

From 1936 to 1939 he served as Editor on Negro Affairs for the Federal Writers' Project; in 1939 he was a staff member of the Carnegie-Myrdal Study of the Negro. He was made a Guggenheim Fellow in 1937. Two of his important works, *The Negro in American Fiction* and *Negro Poetry and Drama,* were published in 1938. In 1941, his landmark anthology, *The Negro Caravan,* was published. *The Last Ride of Wild Bill* appeared in 1975.

Sterling A. Brown has contributed poetry, reviews, and essays to numerous publications. He has also served as visiting professor at Vassar, the University of Minnesota, the University of Illinois (Chicago Circle), and has lectured widely throughout the United States. He has received honorary degrees from University of Massachusetts, Howard University, Northwestern University, Williams College, Boston University, and Brown and Lewis and Clark College.